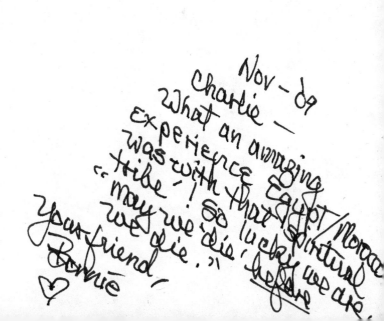

Nov - 09

Charlie —

What an amazing
experience Egypt/Morocco
was with that spiritual
"tribe"! So lucky we die
"may we die" before
we die.."

Your friend,
Bonnie ♡

AM I

I

DEAD

YET?

Bonnie Eddy

Cranky Crones Publishing
Whitefish, MT 59937

AM I DEAD YET?

Bonnie Eddy

Cranky Crones Publishing
Copyright © 2008 by Bonnie Eddy

Cover photo by Pamela Vantress

Author Photo by Sheryl Maree Reily

Cranky Crones
PO Box 1931
Whitefish, MT 59937

ISBN: 978-0-9818264-7-9

Printed in the U.S.A.

This book is dedicated to everyone who opens it.

Thank You

To my editor and best friend, Cindee, for her truthfulness, wisdom, and expertise. For making the book fun to complete. For her praise, encouragement, and support.

To my mom and dad, my son and daughter, my sister, extended family, friends, former husbands/boyfriends, spiritual groups, dogs, and even birds... for giving me the ever so rich life experiences and lessons to be able to grow enough to have something of seeming value and meaning to share with others.

Nothing of the content of this book would have been possible without *all* that has come before.

Thank you.

Table of Contents

"Do not follow where the path may lead. Go instead where there is no path and leave a trail."

(Emerson)

So It Begins

Not writing this book was driving me crazy.

I finally *had* to write it. Put myself out of my misery!

The idea of writing a book was so difficult until I got the experience that 'I' wasn't writing it. It is writing itself *through* me! And, it happens to occur to me, that couldn't *life* work the same way? 'Life' being lived through me?

Well, yeah!

If I let go of the struggle of life because I think 'I' have to do it all, figure everything out that I need to do, out of fear, out of control, out of 'it won't be good enough'... of course, what an awesome task! How will I ever succeed?

But. Like the book writing itself, I don't have to figure out what to write. Think of something new that no one else has ever written. No wonder I postponed and postponed!

I have everything I need. It's just me. It's just about *my* experience of life. It is all right there.

All given.

It has become easy to write this book. Easy to work hard. The saying: "I am choiceless effortless pure awareness" comes to mind.

Writing this is like that.

For a long time - ten years - right after my aunt committed suicide and after my divorce, the book was going to be entitled: *Everything's Perfect. Yeah, but...* (Subtitle: 'An adventure into perceptual reality.')

It was a great book.

Maybe I'll write it someday.

The final sentence was going to be: "Maybe the answer to 'Yeah, but...' is 'SO WHAT?'" The title of the next book would then be: *SO WHAT?* (a further adventure into reality). Or... it's me, it's me, it's me... again.

Then I got carried away.

After *SO WHAT* would be the next book:

GUESS WHAT? It's YOU, again.

Followed by: *WHAT IF?*

Followed by: *WHY NOT?*

And, finally: *NOW WHAT?*

What a series it was! Maybe I don't need to do it again. Actually write it. You see, I have done it once already. In my head, in my dreams.

So, for now, you, the reader, the apparent other, and I will join in sharing a moment in time together with 'this' book.

These writings are about what has been or is true for me today, from my personal experiences. I have found, amusingly so, however, that they *may* not be true for me tomorrow!

The Belated Letter

Running feels good. It gives me time to think and I enjoy hearing the snow squeak under my feet.

It was about time I wrote that thank you letter. I feel such relief. If I'd had a stamp at school, I'd have mailed it on my way home.

My Aunt Nancy, one of my very favorite people, had sent so many things for my birthday two weeks ago. Not just the usual lace panties, but this time also a personalized compact mirror for my purse, a how-to-fold-napkins book, my great-grandmother's hand-carved ivory pen, as well as her miniature opera binoculars, and most especially, a delicate swan made entirely of tiny shells that Nancy had made.

Writing to her always made me feel good. I tell her what's on my mind and know that she listens. This time I told her how much she has always been a role model for me, how her philosophy of living is now mine. I'm anxious for her to receive this letter. Am still puzzled by so many precious presents and ask her about that actually.

I can see her lying on the floor in her living room by the sliding doors that lead out to the almond orchard reading my letter and laughing that great laugh. It is spring there; the trees are probably in full aromatic blossom. Chico in blossom time is my most favorite place on the planet. The whole valley is filled with pink and white, mile after mile, and the aroma is to die for. I once got to fly over the orchards in the helicopter with Dad and experiencing that from the air was ineffable. If I could go anywhere mid-February that will always be where I would go. I imagine Nancy immobilized from back pain lying by the open doors experiencing that grace. And remembering her is always an inspiration.

Every time I try to talk myself out of going running, like today, I see Nancy lying there, knowing she would kill to be able to go running, and I start changing into my grubby clothes and get out the door. I think of her often when I run. I remember when I was a kid that she and my uncle were always late for family affairs, but upon arrival would show their duck or pheasant bounty or don a thoroughly destroyed leather glove as evidence of a glorious day of skiing at Mt. Lassen, one of their lifts being a rope tow. Her laughter is contagious, like that of a delighted infant who has just discovered a mirror in her playpen.

Birds are her true love and my first fear. She sculpts and paints them, mostly ducks and geese, with such depth and clarity and realism that I am afraid to touch the canvas or stand too near. An inherited family phobia. My grandmother used to hang a large feather on the refrigerator to keep the kids out of it. Blue jays would eat out of Nancy's hand and steal through the open door of their creek side camping trailer. I could only touch her pet dove, her house pal of eleven years, if he was being securely held in her trusted hands. She would paint in oils because they didn't drip and she could paint while on the floor. Even on the floor her posture is always so alert. Before her back injury, she carried herself as might a dancing puppet maneuvered by a maestro, magically. The active outdoor life is still indelibly recorded in her slimness, her shining hair, clear skin, and mischievous eyes.

Presents from her were always a surprise. A girl skier in a nose-up fanny-out snow plow with Popsicle stick skis and Q-tip poles with button baskets. Or maybe my great-grandmother's picture frame newly recessed to encase her hand-carved childhood walnut spool dip pen, my great-grandfather's hand-tooled pearl cufflink, a Roosevelt photo campaign button, and a spoon from the San Francisco World's Fair. Once, a laying hen out of dough made entirely from progressively larger and smaller crescent shapes. And now these. The beautiful swan and the sentimental treasures.

Memories flood in. I would do anything for her, even peel potatoes with the scary old cook back in the big kitchen of their coffee shop on First Street when I was a kid. Sometimes, Nancy would weave burgundy velveteen ribbon in my braids and it was just a plain ole day.

And now, I had finished my crisp enlivening run. There was a light snow storm last night, so as long as I am sweaty, I might as well grab the shovel and go clear the back deck while the snow was as light as it was ever going to be.

It was becoming dusk; short daylight hours in the mountains, you know. The sky was beautiful, subdued pastels, wispy clouds, quiet. The snowcats with their familiar and comforting twinkling headlights were beginning to groom the ski slopes.

Mitch, my son, opened the sliding door from the kitchen. "Mom," he called above my scraping shovel, "It's for you. I think it's Papa."

I hope my mom's okay, I thought. They never call this early on a week day.

"Just hand me the phone," I said, removing a wet glove. "I'll talk out here." I pulled the cord as far as I could so I could watch the colors over the western mountains and sat down on the wood pile.

"Hi, Dad. Is everything okay?"

"Well, no, Bonnie. I'm afraid I have some bad news." I could almost see him absently doodling on the yellow pad by his office phone.

An eternity passed, my stomach turning, my heart in suspension.

"Nancy's gone. She died this afternoon."

That can't be, I thought. Her heart was fine. Mom has the heart problem.

"She took her own life, Bonnie. Your mother left for Chico an hour ago."

I felt myself shaking, my throat tightening. I stood up.

"Oh, God..."

My mind was gestalting questions and scenarios. Meltdown was nearing.

"She crawled out into the orchard, dragging her shotgun, and shot herself, Honey."

Silence.

Eternity.

"Are the orchards in blossom?"

"They opened a few days ago," Dad answered in quiet consoling sorrow.

Suicide was not a new subject in Nancy's life. She had discussed it with my mother, her sister, on a few occasions. While I don't advocate suicide, I personally think it is a choice in this reality. That it is naive to consider that it is not. How many of us have given suicide a once over? And I personally do not believe that we are punished for choosing it. Nancy had left a note for my uncle explaining that because of her total immobility now and after years of trying virtually every healing option, she wanted to free him to be able to live a free life. Their prior life. Of hunting, camping, hiking, skiing.

Was it the right choice? Do we immediately regret the decision... too late?

That question was on my mind as I quickly told the kids what had happened. I passed the phone back inside and said that I was going up the hill. Not to worry.

I grabbed our wonderful, beautiful, faithful German Shepherd, my beloved and long time friend, and started climbing up the hill. Far up behind our house and opposite the now-frozen beaver ponds, I climbed through the deep snow to sit on some hay bales that the Forest Service had taken up the gulch for feeding the elk.

I pulled my dog to me and cried, cried, and cried. Mourning so much. Opening that bottomless well of grief we all hold. Grief that Nancy is gone. Grief that life isn't what I thought it would be. Having children, raising children, isn't what I thought it would be. The worry, the exhaustion, the responsibility. That marriage isn't what I thought it would be. The struggle, the nearness, the distance, the unknown future... will it get better?

Grief that grandparents die, aunts die, pets die, parents get sick, I age. I cried it all. I cried until I couldn't feel sorry for myself anymore. That I hadn't written that letter a week ago. The letter sharing so much more than I have shared in the past about how I feel about her, how much I appreciate her, love her. The letter that is right inside my purse. I cried til I was empty, yet strangely full. I cried til I realized it was nearly dark and that I was cold and that my sweet dog's fur was soaked. The pastels had receded, surrendering their softness to night's cold blue and steel gray.

My body continued to go deeper into quietude, felt so uninhabited, yet holy, like being in a magnificent ancient cathedral with no one else there.

I told the dog it was time to go home.

Just then I became aware of movement and to my left and only feet away, a flock of perhaps twenty ducks, from who knows where this time of year, flew by me so near I felt I could reach up and touch them. They made not a sound. They flew with silent wings and silent calls. Were they Nancy's ducks?

And then simultaneously, on my right and at about the same nearness, was my aunt. A shimmering energy and light and her voice. "Bonnie, I love you. I know how you feel about me. Please don't worry. I want you to know I did the right thing. I love you. Always." I was on my feet. Wondrousness. Unspeakable joy and light spilling into me, into whatever I am. Realizing a holy, holy gift, a divine dispensation had just occurred.

My hands cupped my mouth: "I love you, Nancy. I love you, Nancy. I love you, Nancy," ... as I watched, felt, her energy ascending, leaving this silent and most holy of nights.

I walked down the winter slope, the crescent moon rising behind the darkened mountains, joy-filled. The gift received and understood.

My life had just changed.

Irreversibly.

Because I knew.

Irreversibly.

We do not die.

A Birthday Visitation

It was always dark by the time I got home from running in January. It was my birthday and there was a full moon. Had had a good run; not too cold; not too slippery. I was on my way back from running part way up an isolated ravine and stopped, as always, at the place where the creek runs under the road. Love this spot, summer or winter. The dog can get a drink, but more importantly, it is quiet. And the view of Mt. Baldy and the small valley, stunning.

It is where I reflect. Where I solve problems, forgive, go into gratitude before I transition back to house, family, dinner... 'that' life.

Being my birthday, my thoughts naturally flowed to my Aunt Nancy. It has been a year now since her many precious gifts and her suicide. A year since she appeared and spoke to me on the hill not far from here. A year of unbelievable change. Emotionally, becoming more and more who I am, causing even more distancing from my husband. Physically, drinking little, backing out of my co-dependent behavior, attending Al-Anon for help dealing with the dysfunction of alcoholism. Cooking meat only once or twice a week, dropping preparing gourmet meals every night. Simplifying across the board.

Had started traveling to conferences. Self-esteem in education was becoming big. I was gaining expertise for implementing these techniques, as well as accelerated learning skills, into the high school level. Self-esteem-wise, I had unexpectedly discovered that the whole thing was, bottom-line, 'Know Thyself.' And as one does, one will be blown away with one's grandeur, one's beauty. It was much, much deeper than the obvious. And, it was the beginning of my spiritual adventure.

Was not 'asking permission' to take these trips. Just, "Honey, I'm going to be gone." More distancing. The marriage, after twenty-five years, beginning to fall apart because it couldn't change, grow, mature.

But 'I' was.

Changing.

Growing.

Maturing.

Even knowing the probable consequences, I couldn't help myself. I had to. It was survival.

All of these things I was feeling, processing as I stood in the crisp moonlight listening to the magical creek pass beneath my feet. Experiencing the cleansing, healing. Letting the sparkling, dancing water carry my old ways of being away.

Then.

Then I experienced that same acute awareness accompanied by full emptiness and divine quietude as a year ago. Simultaneously, a solitary duck appeared from out of the ravine, flying silently and low. Soon it was about two arm-lengths above me as it suddenly and sharply banked and cut a tight close circle around me. I extended my arm, feeling I might actually be able to touch it. I could feel the energy of its aeronautical feat.

Quiet. Quiet. Quiet.

One we became.

Timelessness was.

A gift. From Nancy. On my birthday. Again, as the duck silently disappeared into the blackness of the ravine: "I love you, Nancy. Thank you, Nancy. I love you."

Unspeakable wonder, gratitude, blessedness as I walked, as on a moonbeam, home. Home to that other life that was also disappearing.

Pee-wee Herman

It had been THE most painful year of my life.

Even seeing it coming, feeling the inevitability. Like death, when a marriage is over, the pain, the shock, the finality cannot be described.

There had been an affair.

How could there not be?

I was no longer who my husband had married. We were strangers.

I would never have left. I was too conditioned, too responsible, too dutiful. He looked like the bad guy. He wasn't. A coward, maybe. Inoperative, maybe. Stuck, immobilized, at the effect of temptation, maybe. But not a bad guy, *the* bad guy.

When the gifts have been given and the lessons learned, does it really matter how it ends? It has to end somehow.

I also was a coward, inoperative, immobilized in terms of not being able to say we have to end this. Now. Honorably.

I just couldn't.

Give up.

Abandon hope.

I loved him.

But it was over. Done.

So, it took a year to settle the divorce. Our righteous egos jumped in. Stuff and money became paramount. We became blind. To love. To forgiveness. To history. To 'being happy' versus 'being right.'

At some point I have read that for atonement to occur, we need to preserve the past in purified form only. Isn't that beautiful? And true? Selective remembering of only the good stuff. It works. It is everything!

As would have it, the divorce papers needed to be recorded at the court house the last day of the month. That would be Halloween. I needed to sign the papers in the morning before work. I was teaching high school and many of us teachers jumped into having fun on that day.

I dressed as Pee-wee Herman. Complete with greased black hair, in a too-small, too-short black suit, bow tie, white socks, black shiny shoes, and rosy cheeks. I had even taped my nose tilted up!

There I was in my husband's attorney's office at 8 a.m., signing the closure of twenty-five years of marriage.

We all cracked up. Hysterically. Uncontrollably. It broke the ice, the division, the opposition.

It was the beginning of healing, of preserving the past, purified.

California Raisins

Speaking of outrageousness and Halloween, several years after my divorce, I was living in Sacramento, teaching 'College Survival' at Sacramento City College. I was becoming quite good at survival. We all are, yes? We seem to still be here!

My daughter was also in Sacramento working for the Sierra Club as a lobbyist. Now there is survival! She was traveling for her job, would be returning October 30th, and I had told her I would pick her up at the airport, at the curb.

My next door neighbor, as luck would have it, was one of these exceptionally creative seamstresses and she always made elaborate costumes for herself and her husband for Halloween. We happened to be having coffee together and it came up. I said, "Wow! Maybe I could borrow one and surprise my daughter at the airport!"

Great idea!

Of the many choices, I chose one of two California Raisin outfits. A deep purple satin puffed and pleated and scalloped affair with an elevated top, a round hole for one's face, and then it tucked in at the thighs. Large padded white gloves, huge sunglasses. I added a pair of black tights, white tennies, and a boombox playing the classic dancing Raisins' song, 'I Heard It Through the Grape-vine.'

I am THE quintessential Raisin.

The next day I don the outfit, grab the boombox and head for the airport. Driving there was inter-esting, but certainly challenging was parking, crossing the parking lot, the busy entry drive, and entering the terminal. All the while dancing to that great song! What's cool about a costume is that nobody knows who you are. It emboldens one. Allows one to be outrageous, courageous. It took me a minute to leave my ego and drop into impersonating, becoming, a perfect Raisin. One to be proud of.

Now this was pre 9/11. No metal detectors. No screening at all. No frisking. You could even walk clear to the gate to meet and welcome your loved ones. Imagine that!

So I did.

Dancing.

The children loved it. Most adults pretended they didn't see me. Hoped I wouldn't approach them. Isn't it sad that we 'adults' (large children who haven't grown up) have forgotten how to play?

So. I am waiting at the gate. Dancing. Embar-rassed.

But nobody knows that.

As soon as Shannon came through the door she saw this dancing Raisin and cracked up. She knew instantly who it was. Why is that, I wonder? Biological connection? Or just Crazy Mother Syndrome.

She loved it. And didn't seem to be embarrassed. In fact, for the next day, the 31st, I borrowed the other Raisin costume and we spent the day dancing through downtown Sacramento.

Raisin' consciousness!

Speaking Of Outrageous

I try to do at least one totally outrageous thing a year.

This 'ritual' began during the years I was consciously working at eliminating fear from my mind.

My life.

I had to develop the art of becoming comfortable being uncomfortable. This was not easy. I had been very conditioned to be a 'good girl,' good person, one who doesn't break the rules. And, one who was always safe.

I took little steps at first.

These may not seem a challenge to someone else.

But this is where I began.

Doing something uncomfortable, for me.

Like:

Brushing my teeth using the other hand. I had huge resistance to even this. 'I' didn't WANT to change. It was easier, faster, to do it the way I was used to doing it.

Sleeping on the other side of the bed. I so got to see how uncomfortable I felt being on the 'wrong' side, the 'other' side.

Having tea instead of coffee. Having mineral water instead of wine. Anything to do with food or drink really rankled my ego self. It was like a parent telling me I couldn't have something. I still have to work on 'Don't tell me what to do!'

Driving someplace a way I've never gone before. Whether to a movie or to a different state.

Going alone to a movie, a museum. What will people think of a woman alone? Can't she get a man?

Spending a weekend alone in an unfamiliar place, like driving to the coast and staying in a B & B! This was huge when I first did it! 'Only couples go to B & B's for a romantic weekend.' More dealing with my stuff and 'Can't she get a man?'

Then I started working up to bigger things.

Some were:

Having a food fight in a restaurant. I know. Wild. I thought I would die. Our group broke the rules, again. (We only attacked our members.) We apologized. We cleaned up the mess. Can't tell you how good it was for me to break a 'good girl' rule like that. The true beginning of my liberation.

Backpacking solo three nights with no dog on Mt. Shasta in an area where most people don't go.

At first my mind tried to take control and scare me, but I have to confess, this ended up *not* feeling like a stretch. I loved the solitude/soulitude.

Telling my parents that whatever it was they wanted me to do really didn't work for me.

"Thank you for inviting me, but coming down this weekend doesn't work for me."

Building my own house. Insisting on curved walls even if the contractor thinks I'm nuts.

Moving to a new town alone. I left where I had lived for ten years and moved to Montana.

Traveling alone to Croatia for an International Peace Conference.

Traveling alone to Bhutan to meet and trek with friends.

In the Enneagram, I am a Counterphobic Six (already sounds ominous, doesn't it?). Unlike Phobic Six, where fear immobilizes, Counterphobic Six steps repeatedly into the lion's mouth to prove they are *not* afraid.

Being a Counterphobic Six might help? But I really don't think so. I think our basic human nature, generally, is to be safe and secure.

Comfortable.

Not venture.

Alone.

But I tell you...

Outrageousness?

Doing the unexpected, the unaccepted?

Very juicy, indeed.

Even 'naughty.'

And, THAT'S very fun.

Thank You, Mom

Letting go. Letting go. Why is that so difficult?

That we don't trust, have faith, in the void, the unknown?

My mom was utterly terrified during her dying process. I, curiously and with divine perfection surely, was the only one in her sphere who could, would, did, step up with my limited knowledge or first-hand experience of dying and risk everything, including being wrong, to assuage her fear. I would have done anything to comfort her during this time.

I trusted myself more in midwifing Mom in her dying process than I ever have in my life. Opened myself. Made myself more vulnerable than ever. Listened and trusted what I got, and acted. Courageously.

Will I ever know, for sure, that it was right for Mom? For me?

I have to trust that it was. That the soul *does* travel up through the energy centers and leaves through the top of the crown. That there *is* warm light. That if you get frightened or lost, you can ask for help, and angels, guides, *are* there. Instantly. That it's like swimming under water, but you *can* breathe.

Was it, Mom? Was it that way?

God... I hope so.

I did for her what I thought 'I' would want. What I hope someone will do for me.

'Feather' my body. Give me soft facial touch with a deep red velvet rose. Give hand rubs, foot rubs. Lightly touch my chakras in sequence up to my crown, reminding my soul of the way. Prepare my crown for the exit of my soul by gently cupping upward, a continued reminder. Sing: "You're an angel, you're a being of light, you're an angel and I know that I'm right." Softly whisper in my ear: You are good, you are kind, you are love, you are light, you are God, you are everything that is, you are peace, you are beautiful, you have lived such a beautiful life, you have done such beautiful things, you are so loved by me, by everyone; you are safe, you are safe, you are safe; you are protected, you are protected, you are so loved and protected. Peace, peace. All is well, all will be well.

When I die, stay with me and tell me everything is okay. Tell me what will happen to my body now, where I am going, and remind me that I will need to trust yet again and soon leave for my next step... to return home. See my God light, my agony and ecstasy of love, rather than my empty and possibly old worn out body. Tell me that you will invite me to visit often. Look for me in reflecting light in the water, in the clouds, and trust that

I am there still loving you. Because I will be, Mitch. I will be, Shannon. I will be.

Mom, are you there? Loving me still?

I feel that you are. I feel that you are a very near guide now and that I shared so deeply my dreams and love that you are guiding me in right action. I feel your quiet presence. See you in my dreams. And... miss your physical presence so.

The last week before she went into coma prior to dying, when the nurse would ask if she needed the bedpan, she would say, "Might as well, can't dance." (Which she adored doing.) Then she would pretend to play the piano and start to sing Frank Sinatra's, "I won't dance, don't ask me..." That was my cue to dance around the room to her accompaniment. We would laugh and laugh. And cry. We were like ten-year-old best friends.

How sweet, flirtatious, demure, innocent, lovable she became. What a gift she gave me... to see who we 'really' are without all our masks; the idea of why not be that person NOW rather than wait til death's call. Be who we are NOW. Be that innocent, lovable, trusting, joyful, beautiful, play-ful child NOW!

Mom, in your dying process, I have never loved more, never better. Is that what vulnerability, let-ting go, trusting creates?

What a precious, precious gift you have given me, Mom.

Thank you.
Thank you.
Thank you.
Thank you.
Thank you.
Thank you.
Thank you.
Thank you.
Thank you.

The Ring

Mom had always wanted a beautiful diamond ring.

Had waited years for Dad to buy her one. Especially after the business became successful... enough.

She even bought him one.

He didn't 'get it.' Didn't get how important it was to her.

Until.

Until she was diagnosed with terminal lung cancer and she went out and bought it for herself.

It really was a stunning ring. A two carat emerald cut with pure clarity set in an unusual, but elegant and exquisite gold setting. The perfect ring.

Mom loved it. Wore it to the very end. Can still see her admiring it on her finger in the hospital, especially when the sun would come in and it would catch its light and send rainbows around the room. She had it for six months.

The ring has taught me a lot.

Not to wait.

For anything you might want to do. Want to have. Want to be.

We don't know how long we will be here. If something is important, do it. Have it. Be it. Now.

The ring did, however, pose its own set of 'problems.'

Who was to have it when Mom died?

Choices: My older sister. Me. One of my sister's three daughters. My daughter.

When Mom and Dad went to their estate attorney to set things in order, they gifted it to my daughter for the future. How do you split a ring three ways, between my sister's daughters, being the rationale. In the meantime, I was given the ring to wear until I died. My sister given a gorgeous family heirloom ring Mom had had redesigned and embellished. Gorgeous. But not a two carat emerald cut diamond.

Great. Now there was guilt to be dealt with. Guilt and the challenge of dropping my previous judgments about women who wore 'those' kinds of rings.

Now 'I' get to be one of 'those' women who wear 'those' kinds of rings?!

I even tried to give it to my sister! She wore it for a couple of weeks and was so worried about losing it or having it stolen or being mugged that she gave it back.

Finally, I worked through my stuff enough to start wearing it. It does draw attention. So that takes getting used to. And truly, "What will people think of me?" was ever present in the early times of wearing it. I don't wear it when I travel. Just don't want to have to think about it.

Maybe some women who wear those kinds of rings just think they are beautiful and want that experience. Maybe some women who wear those kinds of rings inherit them from mothers whose dream it was to own something stunning like that.

Maybe it doesn't matter.

Doesn't mean anything.

Owning those kinds of rings.

Like everything else.

Maybe it's just me. Me giving everything all the meaning it has.

I have to point to myself. Again.

It's me. Again.

Surprise surprise.

And I do love the ring. It's my mom's. I see her light in it.

My light in it.

Your light in it.

Phew... I Made It

Isn't it interesting that we spend so much - all? - of our lives trying to survive so that we can be relieved on our death bed that we 'made it?!'

Maybe this is a futile attempt at expressing the inexpressible.

But.

I watched my father... I *could* use me, and may... but, right now, I'll use him.

I watched my father, after Mom died, go to heroic lengths to finally 'make it' to his death bed.

He pool exercised, often twice a day, even in 58-degree water to 'outsmart,' to 'beat,' the effects of Parkinson's, the effects of the aging body of a 90-plus-year-old. He had regular deep body work with a friend of mine which often left him exhausted. He went to physical therapy. He begged his neurologist to let him be a guinea pig for experimental brain surgery. He would have done *anything* to prolong 'making it' to his death bed.

Bless his heart.

How I miss this man. Love this man. Because of this I think he is with me more than when he was here.

One talks about 'Keep on keeping on.' He was the king of keep on keeping on. He was the model for 'passion for life.'

How could I possibly judge him?

Why would I?

Did I?

Yes.

I did.

Near the end. Certainly, the last year.

Dad, let go. Give it up. You won't win this battle.

It was heartbreaking.

SO much will to live. Like the new young tree growing out of the seemingly dead stump.

Reasons to live. The last one: Buy a new helicopter for the business. It wasn't about rationale. It was about a reason to live. Something to look forward to. He could sit in it. He could be a passenger in it. Heart-wrenchingly, he could not fly it.

I think he ran out of reasons to perpetuate himself:

Burt, the quintessential pilot.
Burt, the quintessential employer.
Burt, the generous father, grandfather, great-grandfather.
Burt, the willing guinea pig.
Burt, the battler of Parkinson's.
Burt, the battler of aging.
Burt, the buyer of new helicopters.

What happened?

Was it running out of reasons?

Did he finally just get tired?

Finally see the futility?

Make a decision to stop?

Stop trying to 'make it' to the death bed?

Let whatever 'Burt' was, go?

Bless his heart.
Bless his heart.
Bless his heart.

Bless *our* hearts.

Bless *my* heart.

Bless *your* heart.

Is this the 'die before you die?'

I think so.

Yes.

Can I?

Die before I die?

Stop?

Quit trying to 'make it?'

⊗ℰ

My daughter just called. I read *Phew* to her.

We cried.

Would anyone else reading this cry?

Our pain, the pain of *loving*, is the same for us all. The names, the events and the story don't matter.

It is *loving* that we feel.

The pain and ecstasy of *loving* that we share.

That binds us.

"Well, Guys, I'm Going to Die Tonight"

It was February 16th. I had driven back home to Mt. Shasta after my sister had picked Dad up at the airport office and taken him down to Chico for the weekend.

Dad, at 94, still actively ran the helicopter business he and mom had founded fifty years earlier. He only recently quit driving and then only because of a small stroke. And my sis and I had insisted. (It's the pits to be the bad cop.) Parkinson's was gradually taking its toll on his body, balance in motion being the greatest problem. He had fallen a couple of times, once breaking his hip, the classic story, and we thought: "This will be the beginning of the end."

It wasn't.

His recovery and his will were nothing short of miraculous. He was back to work quickly, but finally, reluctantly, condescending to use a walking stick (Mom's gorgeous hand-carved natural wood one) at work and a walker at home, in privacy. A proud man he was. He was actually extraordinarily fit and healthy, pool exercising well into the autumn. Only a Scorpio would enjoy this! He hated to give up this beloved early morning ritual.

Witnessing Dad's determination to 'combat' the inevitable decline of his body (bodies just seem to finally wear out... like everything else in this temporal reality), witnessing his aging process has made the decline of my own body somehow easier, somehow allowing me more grace and acceptance (twisted toes and aberrant gray hair excluded!).

My sister and I, the last year or so, had been going to Redding every week to help out at the business and at Dad's home. He still preferred to live alone (again, Scorpio that he was), and managed remarkably well.

There was such a delicate, fragile balance to be sought in all this. A high, high degree of honoring. The truest guide for me in witnessing, in assisting in my father's aging transition was to remember to constantly ask myself: What would 'I' want? What *will* I want? How *will* I want to be treated? Not as a child, but as a wise, aware person who has accumulated untold life experience; a fragile human being to be honored, respected and supported in ending a life well lived.

I will get back to February 16th in a moment.

My father modeled 'highest good for the greatest number' long before I could put words to his deeds. He was an exceptional employer - *the* ideal employer - treating his employees as surrogate family. Most of the mechanics, pilots, and drivers had been with Dad for many, many years.

Some, thirty-five years. I think actually he was, in fact, a surrogate father figure to everyone there. His business, a model, a paradigm for functional, equitable, mostly consensus decision making. "What do you think we ought to do here, guys?" ('Guys' included Brenda, our godsend of an office manager, and occasionally included opinions or input from the wives.)

I don't think I fully realized... Scratch that. In my own spiritual arrogance, I did *not* realize to what degree my father was a true sage. (I'm so evolved, ya know.) How humbling. How embarrassing. Forgive me, everyone. Anyone whom I have burdened with this demeanor. I am so, so sorry.

It wasn't until Dad's memorial at the hangar at the airport on a cool showery March day that I realized his evolved soul.

Nearly three hundred people attended. Attended a 94-year-old private man's memorial. A man whose contemporaries, siblings, aged relatives had all died. (I think here of the handful or so of people who would probably show up at mine, speaking of spheres of influence!)

My sister and I officiated. It was a 'family affair' in every greater definition of that word. A huge number of attendees were from Dad's Forest Service, Fish and Game, or Bureau of Land Management families. From his timber, rancher, agriculture, television, and private families. From families we didn't even know existed.

After grandkids had shared many wonderful memories with this bereaved group, the general sharing started: "He was my model for being a man. My surrogate father. He loaned me money. He saved my life. He taught me how to fly. He flew my first smoke jump. I trusted my life to him. He was the most generous man I ever met..."

The Forest Service had an honor guard. We were presented with their flag, framed; a rare honor to a private individual. They had also made a large framed plaque with wonderful early pictures of Dad in his first helicopter, a B2, with the following inscription, his motto for living, for doing business, which he had cut from a *Reader's Digest* years before and carried in his wallet:

Is it the truth?
Is it fair to all concerned?
Will it build goodwill and better friendships?
Will it be beneficial to all concerned?
                              (Anonymous)

Sounds like the highest good for greatest number to me!

A second framed plaque is hanging in the Redding Airport terminal in his honor.

Dad's memorial gathering was a great spiritual event. We were all taken out of ordinary time and space. Quite honestly, like when sitting with the

Dalai Lama or Ammachi. We became one. There was no separation. Wives of attendees approached in tears saying they hadn't met Dad, but they couldn't stop crying.

Love was, literally, in the air. No one wanted to leave (... like THE best wedding ever).

Couldn't we stay in this love space forever? The memory of that day is, gratefully, with me still. I only have to think about it to reactivate the energy.

Thank you, Dad. Thank you, God.

Thank you. Thank you. Thank you.

⊗⊗⊗

Back to February 16th.

In Chico, my sister, brother-in-law, and Dad had just finished dinner.

Dad pushed himself back from the table and announced: "Well, guys, I'm going to die tonight."

In that instant, all his physical and emotional strength, his health and his will to live left. They carried him to the recliner. My sister called me in Mt. Shasta, stunned, numbed by the spontaneous and definitive change. "He's dying, Bonnie. He can hardly speak."

They talked to him, massaged him, told him what he could not voice: "We know you love us. We know you're grateful for all our help in the past. We'll tell everyone goodbye for you. And thank you, thank you for all you have been for us, done for us. We love you so."

He drifted off.

Woke with a start: "Am I dead yet?"

Three times he did this.

(My exhilaration upon hearing: I knew it! I knew it! I just knew we couldn't tell the difference. I just knew it. Thank you, Dad. Thank you for this final gift.)

They carried him to bed.

It was frost warning time for the almond blossoms and my brother-in-law got up at 3 a.m. to check the orchards. Dad was sleeping on his side quietly, gently snoring.

When checking on him at 4:15, he was gone.

Was he a Bodhisattva? Three intentional breaths and you're gone? A decision made?

Maybe.

Probably.

Yes.

Why *not* Dad?

Why *not* me?

Why *not* you?

Papa Sightings

While in Baja, I received this email from my daughter-in-law. My granddaughter, Stella, is four years old. 'Papa' was my dad, Burt.

"Stella and I were at Mrs. Spoonover's having an ice cream yesterday and she was facing the counter and had been staring over there for some time. Then she said, 'Look, Mama, there is a man we love sitting at the counter.'

"I turn around and I do not see anyone. I said, 'Stella, I don't see anyone. Who is it?'

"She looks at me funny and says matter-of-factly, 'It is Papa Burt, silly!'

"I said, 'Oh, what is he wearing?'

"And she perfectly described him in his pressed jeans, cowboy boots and favorite short-sleeved pink shirt.

"Amazing."

What can one say?

Stella has had many dreams about Dad that she shares when she climbs in bed with her parents in the morning.

"Last night Papa flew into my room in a little tiny helicopter."

And what happened then? "We talked."

What do you talk about? "Stuff."

I love it. I believe it.

My dad showed up outside my office window as an unusually huge, big, fat, somewhat unreal, hummingbird a few days after the memorial, during a major spring snowstorm!

I kid you not! Who else would come and 'hover' like a helicopter during a snowstorm?

Why Not?

Go to Machu Picchu?
Move to Montana?
Travel in a Vanagon?
Invite my son and family to live in my house?
Spend three months in Baja in the winter?
Go to Guatemala?
Contribute money?
Buy a tiny piece of property in a foreign country?

What would stop me? Only fear.

Fear of what?

Not enough? Oh, *that* again?

Might die? Oh, *that* again?

What if:

This is my only time in a human body?
I had regrets?
I'm not really here?
I don't really exist?
I'll never 'know' for sure, have total certainty?

What would stop a 'Why not?'

Only a 'What if?'

I say: "So what!"

So What?

So what?

If my computer crashed?
If I don't have Skype?
If I can't easily be in contact?
If I'm afraid? Of love, of God, of being what I am,
of …?

So what?

Wow! Where does that question leave me?

Speechless. Yes!

An ego knockout. Yes!

So what?

If my parents are gone and I miss them?
If I worry about financial survival, my long-term
health?
If this world is literally falling apart, is insane?
If humanity hates humanity, is mean-spirited?

So what?

"Get over yourself!" (as a popular exclamation
goes).

It does sound unfeeling, noncompassionate. But, truly, honestly, rock-bottom-face-it truth, isn't it the last question?

What do I do with 'So what?'

Besides 'Keep on keeping on.'
Besides 'Do the best you can with the awareness you have.'
Besides 'Trust. Trust that all is in some kind of divine chaotic order. That our higher selves are in cahoots. Or not.'
Besides "Bonnie, relax, quit trying to figure *anything* out."
Besides 'Just *have* this experience called life? Don't judge it or fix it. Just *have* it.'
Besides 'Abandon hope.'

Is this easy to do?

No!

So what?

What We Can Count On Is.....

NOTHING!

Lucy

Lucy is a dog.

Lucy is a Mexican dog. A very tubular dog.

Lucy is the sister of Desi, who is no longer with us.

She was never trained. She comes when you call her. Immediately. Happily. Enthusiastically.

She leads the pack when the 'walking girls and dogs' go walking. She glides along seemingly effortlessly. Like those amazing large bodied friends who dance or ski as if on wings.

Lucy smiles. She seems to say: "I am so happy to see you, to be with you,"... with her whole being.

What a joy to experience her, to take care of her, be her 'dog person' for a moment in time. I feel so privileged, so special.

"I LOVE LUCY."

A Bump Up

The highest good for all...

That is an elevated consideration to add to one's decision-making process. (I thought I used it all the time.)

Is building my house the highest good for all? Is going to my dad's this weekend the highest good for all? Or is going camping? Is contribution to this cause the highest good for all? Is having my son and family live in my house (while their own is being built) the highest good for all?

Take that last question, for example. Would 'all' imply *my* highest good, or just *their* highest good?

I had a major bump up into recognizing my still-strong ego when I heard the following addendum: Highest good for the *most* people, for the *greatest* number.

I invite you to ask yourself *that* question and watch *your* ego's reaction.

My first reaction was startlingly obvious to me: "Oh... well, uh... I didn't mean being *that* generous, *that* unselfish."

When I asked that question regarding my house/my son and family, there was a hands-down no doubt as to the answer.

I was new to town. Knew, mostly, only extended family. My son Mitch, and Amy, his wife, have a huge sphere of influence, in my mind, in their community. Mitch's work, chef, food rep, as well as ski involvement. Amy's work, an attorney as well as school board member. They seem to be a grounding rod for other married couples with and without children and have an active social life, to say nothing of two older German Shepherd dogs and an old cat. Amy was seven months pregnant with their second child. Their daughter, Stella, a secure four-year-old.

The ripple effect of just what I could see for their being provided a secure living environment was impressive. The highest good for the greatest number? Obvious.

Then, later, while traveling, part of the impetus to take a bit of a risk in buying a tiny lot in Baja, was asking myself that question. Seeing the far-reaching possibilities for service and generosity in my own life, in my own 'sphere of influence.'

I often wonder what our world would look like today if our President, our governing bodies, asked this question when tough decisions needed to be made.

If *all* people in power on the planet asked this question. If people in power of oil, of water, of fishing, of timber, of education.

But it starts with *me*.

With *you*.

A Healed Mind Does Not Plan

"A healed mind does not plan." (Lesson 135 of *A Course In Miracles*)

I finally get this... but can I *talk* about it?

What helped me was practicing living 'my strategy' from the Human Design System (a complex system of self-exploration using astrology, but primarily the I Ching). In that system I am a Projector, and a Projector's strategy is to "wait for the delicious invitation"... for anything (career, moving, relationship, day-to-day activities).

So I practiced waiting. Actually, more so, 'waiting without waiting.' Somewhere in the past I had read that in waiting without expectation, your real life appears. But you cannot come to this through 'wanting' it because then it is merely a repetition of your memory! I think that is true and actually very cool. Anyway, as I practiced, I discovered that I did not *have* to plan, did not *have* to figure out my life. Spontaneity, serendipity, began to occur with more and more frequency.

I was in Montana for four days over Easter two years ago to see my then four-year-old granddaughter. I had seriously thought about moving to the area when Dad died, but had made no plans or investigations around it. We were walking our favorite circuit through a neighborhood I had connected with in the past, of mostly large, expensive homes. But this day there was a For Sale sign on one of the few small homes. The house was charming, beckoning. I called the realtor. The sign had just gone up and the house had been on MLS for only twenty minutes. I saw it. And I bought it. Utterly delicious!

Another example. I had, in the most distant past when making lists of what I wanted, included seeing Machu Picchu as well as speaking fluent Spanish. As the years had passed, I had let these go. "Oh, it isn't that important."

Well, I was in Hanalei, Hawaii, for a wedding and called a girlfriend back on the mainland while on an early beach walk to tell her I was on her favorite beach. In the course of this conversation she said, "Hey, I'm going to Peru with my favorite traveling buddies. Why don't you come with us!" Felt delicious. I said yes, not knowing a thing about the trip. It was one of the most profound experiences of my life. Need I say more?

Probably not.

But I will.

Prior to this, I had moved into that house in Montana and shortly after decided to let my son and his young family plus dogs and a cat live there while they built their own home. It was winter. I yearned for sun. And, I admit, a little solitude. I had been in touch with a new friend who had a rental in Mt. Shasta (I had given her an emergency astrological reading a few years ago). She spends winter in Baja; her description had been very 'inviting.' I called to tell her I thought I might go down. I contacted a property management person in Baja. Rentals were pretty pricey for one person. Then I got an e-mail from Pamela, my friend in Mt. Shasta, saying some friends had a casita for a really good price. I called. It worked. I sent a deposit for three months!

I had not planned to have a car down there, just walk everywhere. My casita landlord said that it would be pretty difficult, everything was spread out. The next day Pamela happened to mail again and said, "By the way, you'll need a car. I have a friend with two. She'll rent you one. She'd like the extra income. Here is her e-mail."

What is that miracle?

Can I, can anyone, trust 'putting it out there'... and then waiting?

I think so. Yes.

Maybe it's part of the quickening that we all feel. That 'There used to be twenty-four hours in a day, but now there are only twenty,' feeling. That 'I think it and it manifests almost immediately.' i.e. "You'll want a car." Then an e-mail offering one.

Positive or 'negative' manifestation. Someone coughs or sneezes in the seat next to you. Fear: "Oh God, I hope I don't get sick... and..."

I've strayed a bit.

Surprise, surprise.

A healed mind does not plan. Maybe it is the 'Let go, let God' idea. That old 'If you want to hear God laugh, make plans,' joke.

We can make plans, certainly, but I think the caveat is: Be totally willing to let them go; to change them; postpone them; drop our agendas.

That old 'attachment' issue.

That old 'Would you rather be right or happy?' idea.

That old 'I'll die, if this doesn't happen'... 'if I can't have...'

Hmm... Is this that old 'Die before you die' thing again? I see.

I may not *like*.

But I *do* see.

The Remember-er

My dad, the last ten or so years of his life, would complain of his loneliness, his aloneness, even despair. His siblings were gone. His wife was gone. Almost all contemporaries were gone, his WWII pilot friends.

I didn't understand. Even in my supposed empathy, I didn't really understand.

I would go down on 'my' weekends. We would visit the one, maybe two, friends left. Would drive to MacArthur Falls for breakfast at Hal & Kathy's. Drive loops to re-explore old haunts. Even go to Fields or French Glen in southeastern Oregon where he and Mom worked for eleven glorious, exciting summers.

Listen to music from his era, watch movies from his era. Re-live memories.

A fleeting gratification. 'Almost' the experience.

But.

Not quite.

I didn't understand the sadness, the letting go, the heartbreak, the acceptance of something one can not change.

But now.

Now.

I turned 66 a few weeks ago.

Some of my contemporaries are dying.

My former husband and dear friend for twenty-five years... Gone.

My mom. My dad.

Who do I talk to about those shared memories? Those memories so rich with juicy life experience, so rich with love, joy, sorrow, triumph.

The birth of a son. A daughter.

Twenty-five years of shared life:

Courtship.
College craziness.
Wedding, honeymoon.
Risk-taking.
Buying our first house.
Deciding to have a baby; getting a puppy first!
Moving to the East Coast; then to Idaho.
Backpacking to every available and unavailable lake with the kids.
Surprise 40th birthday party in San Francisco.
Surprise birthday trip to Hawaii (first time there).
Death of parents, of friends, of dogs.

I'm beginning to understand.

I don't think it would have mattered even if I had understood when Dad was alive.

It is a solo journey. This journey into heartache. This journey of allowing my self to die. Slowly disappear.

Until finally, no one remembers the memories, the remember-er.

Can I say 'So what' to this?

Not easily.

Not without pain.

Not without asking: "Did that life, *my* life, matter?"

What was it for?

Love

Love.

I think it was, is, only for love.

It is only the loving moment, pain or ecstasy, that has value for me... anymore. That feels real to me.

I remember those gone, my husband, my mom, my dad, and the remembering is so filled with the pain, with the ecstasy, of love.

AND, it is absolutely no different from remembering, from thinking about, my son, my daughter, a grandchild, a dear friend, a brief precious encounter in a grocery line or on a flight.

I just love.

I love to love.

I *love* love.

God's Goof

I don't recall where I first heard this story of the original separation, but I love it and think it is helpful, certainly to me, for getting an inkling of some understanding of our original imprinting and its subsequent behavioral consequences.

It goes something like this: *Once upon a time*, in the beginning before time and space, God had a thought and that thought was, "Wouldn't it be nice to experience 'other' and, therefore, 'all of my self?' And to let all those parts of me experience them selves *as* me?" A gift, actually.

Well, because of the omnipotence of God's creative energy, before God (also known as the Absolute, Reality, fill in the blanks) knew what had happened, the Big Bang was birthed and all time and space - past, present, future - simultaneously occurred. God instantly realized the error and corrected it almost as it seemed to occur. What was left was only an impression, an illusion of what seemed, for a trillionth of a second, to have occurred.

How you and I, now seemingly separate consciousnesses, experienced what was meant to be a beautiful gift, was shocking instead - like the harshness of birth from the womb. You and I, sensing our supposed separateness, believed we had been abandoned, betrayed, left on our own;

lone souls 'kicked out' of 'heaven,' where everything was only and in all ways one thing, one experience of divine love; an 'Of this I cannot
speak' experience because it *was/is* truly ineffable.

So we (whatever we think we are), were deeply
imprinted with that experience of relationship, of
duality, of two things, and we carry that uncon-
sciously into every relationship we have. That
suspicion. That dis-ease. That non-trusting.
"When is the other shoe going to drop?" When is
'other'... other anything, 'gonna get me.'

We armor. Somewhere our cells remember that
belief of abandonment, that trillionth-of-a-second
memory that was simultaneously reversed. But
somewhere our cells also remember from
whence we came and to which we will return. To
Source... whatever it is, whatever you want to
call it.

The cosmic joke, painful but true, is that it really
never happened. We only 'think' it did. Individu-
ally and collectively. And we experience life after
apparent life because of that thought. "I think,
therefore, I am," stuff.

Because of that I perpetuate my apparent life experiences, apparent subsequent karma, and appear to have to keep coming back and cleaning
up the mess I made last time!

Good grief. Isn't that amazing?

I thought so, when the reality first dawned on me. Was stunned speechless actually. Hit so literally I couldn't find myself, my body, anywhere. Had a very difficult transition 'back.' Really didn't want to return. From the Tao. From the unbelievably beautiful full emptiness that is so 'Home.'

I am, however, pretty sure that I had mucked things up before enough that I *had* to come back. Like that witticism, "God gave me so much to do this time, I'll probably never die!"

I have heard that if our ego dies, karma ends. Even knowing all this - and I have great certainty (though I have learned that 'certainty' is a dangerous thing) of its truth, and enough experiences which validate for me that this physical reality is an illusion, a paper tiger - even knowing this, I'm afraid to love. To open to possible abandonment.

Even knowing that the only true reality, the blank canvas upon which my apparent life is painted, is love, I am afraid.

Even practicing living with love – "Is this a loving thought, a loving idea, a loving action?" I'm afraid. Afraid to be what I already am.

There is hope for me though because 'my world' is becoming less and less fear-filled. Less and less 'of' this world. My world is more and more feeling like the 'Home' I somewhere, somehow, remember and trust.

You're Kidding, Right?

The question – "You're kidding, right?" - popped up seriously for me less than two weeks ago.

This was the series of events.

My father's house was sold at long last and $70,000 below appraisal value, in escrow with an 'as is' condition because I had lowered the price so much. December 30th the buyers did a roof inspection. Were told it would need to be replaced in a year or two for $5,000. They wanted me to pay for it. What does 'as is' mean, anyway? The deal fell through.

Another man whose agent showed him the house after dark and managed, God only knows how, to fall off the pool deck behind huge potted redwood trees and cement decorative benches, is now not only suing for medical expenses, but also loss of wages (I can understand these), pain and suffering (he broke his arm and collar bone... don't laugh, Bonnie), and is now just plain suing me. You're kidding, right?

Meantime, I am scheduled to leave for a well-deserved R & R in Baja on January 11th. My son, daughter-in-law, four-year-old granddaughter, and five-week-old baby granddaughter are living in my Montana house while their own home is being built. Oh, and their two German Shepherd dogs and monstrous-sized cat (all three of which I adore actually). But we all needed some space and time apart. Imagining this does not take any explanation.

I had been having occasional spontaneous dizzy spells (from a concussion resulting from a rear-end accident in 2005?); loss of hearing and affected balance system in my right ear from a viral infection three years ago (or maybe a divine download of light and wisdom from the All-Omnipotent? Take your pick.) At any rate, the week before I am to leave, I have three spells in a row, then finally a serious one where I could not get out of bed (this after hearing I was being sued). It is Friday. My daughter-in-law, with two kids in tow, comes, gets me and drives me to the doctor. An MRI is ordered for Monday afternoon. I am to leave for Baja on Thursday.

Because I am going to be gone until the end of March, I need to get my tax info together as best I can. In 2006 my father has died, his helicopter business sold, I had hoped his home sold, but not yet; I left the perfect house and landscape I had built in Mt. Shasta; I bought a house in Montana, sold two cars (don't ask) and I'm sure there is more. But isn't that enough? SO. After entering December information into Quicken, Monday a.m. is the suspenseful day to hit the magic 'tax summary' button. I did. And only August through December appeared! You really have *got* to be kidding. I had bought a new computer around July; a friend transferred everything from old to new for

me. Or not. Gratefully, I had backed up everything from my old computer on a zip. However –
how can this happen? - the zip drive ate up the
zip. Clever Calvin, my miracle computer guy,
saved the zip. The drive was toast. Sooo, I call
Calvin who is about twenty miles south, and he
says to bring the zip down; he'll transfer it to a
disk for me.

I am leaving for Baja Thursday morning at 6 a.m...
I need to pack and a gazillion other things.

I arrive for my MRI at 1 p.m. and spend the most
cacophonous one hour and fifteen minutes of my
life inside a tube with my head inside a cage.
Mustn't move, Bonnie. I request country western
music (thought about Christian, just in case, but
then thought: what the hell, live dangerously).
Never heard it over the jackhammer ensemble.

I get out of the hospital shell-shocked and drive
to Clever Calvin who does his magic and we load
the disk to make sure I have January to August.
We do. God is good.

By now Monday is slipping away. I leave for Baja
at 6 a.m. Thursday.

Tuesday is my son's 40th birthday. (Is this why
I'm dizzy?)

I awaken Tuesday dizzy, can not get out of bed,
take a vertigo pill and promptly crash. (Side effects: drowsiness/sleepiness. A gross under-

statement.) Four hours later I am awake and able to get a shower. I was supposed to 'help' Amy at their just-newly-enclosed house for a birthday and family dinner party. I get out of the shower and four-year-old Stella has a surprise for me. I close my eyes and when told to turn around and open my eyes there is my beautiful daughter, Shannon, who had emailed Monday from Sacramento saying she *wasn't* going to be able to come! What a sweet treat her appearance is.

I now have Wednesday to get everything done. I am leaving for Baja at 6 a.m. Thursday.

The party, thanks to Amy's creativity, is a wonderful, wonderful event filled with sweet family sentiment. (She is throwing a 'roast' party with Mitch's friends Saturday night at a cross country ski retreat.) 'I' will be in Baja.

Shannon and I are talking after the party about using Skype for calling while I'm in Baja. I had signed up Monday and she was going to show me how to use it. I am grateful.

The Skype I signed up for (skype-free calls.com, or something likely-sounding) is a fake website, a scam. We are up til 2 a.m. cancelling my Visa card because I had provided all of my card info. It is now Wednesday. (Did I mention that I was put on an antibiotic Monday? Stella had come down with strep the day we were all baking cookies, licking frosting from fingers, etc.)

Not to worry.

I still haven't heard how the MRI came out. I *am* leaving for Baja at 6 a.m. tomorrow morning. I may die in Baja. I decide to get travel insurance.

We go on-line to download my boarding pass. The printer is out of ink. Should I be surprised?

I had organized my ride from the airport in Cabo to Todo Santos, where my little casita is waiting. I receive word that that has changed. I would now need to take a shuttle from the airport to the bus terminal and take a bus. (By now, I am not surprised.)

Since I am going to be gone for three months and my car, which is white, is brown (that is just the way winter is in Montana) AND, it is nearly 30 degrees out so the locks shouldn't freeze, I decide to go get the car washed for storage.

Stella has almost filled her 'chore chart' with stars, the reward being for all of us to go see *Charlotte's Web* together. It is the last day it's playing. It is a delightful film. Go see it. Take tissue.

(The clock is ever ticking.)

We come out of the theater. It is dark. I leave in a few hours. I pack. I take too much. Do I care? There is a phone message at home: MRI is clear.

Up at 4 a.m. Very dark, sub-zero, my son drives Shannon and me to the airport. There by 5 a.m. Her flight is on Delta to Salt Lake at 6 a.m.; mine is on Horizon to Seattle at 6 a.m. I arrive at the counter. The flight last night could not get in, reasons unknown, therefore the 6 a.m. flight has been cancelled. (Refer here to the title of this story.) I am put on standby on my daughter's flight to Salt Lake. They are concerned about weight because it is snowing in SLC and they need to take on extra fuel for circling due to delays. Telling them I only weigh 120 pounds didn't help. (They didn't know my luggage weighed 85!) I go to the end of that line to get my possible ticket. Maybe Shannon and I will be able to sit together, I think. (Silly me.) We go through our first check-in. I am taken aside and told I have been chosen for 'closer inspection' or whatever they call it. (Should I be surprised by any of this at this point?) I pass.

Actually I make standby probably because I was a solo passenger. A kind cowboy (seriously, we're in Montana, ya know) gave Shannon his seat by me. We have a quality hour flight. It is snowing, but no circling. Shannon runs to her flight, a tight connect. I, with my three hour layover, leisurely buy a Starbucks soy latte and stroll three terminals over to my gate. It is 9:30. I buy a bowl of hot soup for breakfast. I am dressed for Baja. It is 11 a.m.; we leave at 11:20. Our plane has not arrived. I receive a call from Shannon thinking she has arrived in Sacramento.

She is three terminals away waiting to take off. (See title.)

At 11:30 our plane arrives and we are told after a quick crew change, fueling, and loading we will be on our way. Fifteen minutes later it is announced that this plane has 'clock' problems and that the technicians cannot correct it. (Refer to title.) They are getting another plane to the gate. "Go get something to eat and be back at 12:15." Five minutes later, it is announced that the clocks have actually been fixed. "Go help find the passengers who fled to get something to eat. We are leaving in ten minutes." (See title.) We board and leave the gate at 12:30. It is still snowing. We are de-iced with a pink caustic shower and line up with the other flamingos. At 1:15 we're still on the tarmac, but number three to go, we are de-iced again. The thought that I am heading for Baja is ever present. We take off at 1:30. Thank you, God.

We land at 4:30 p.m. It is raining. (Refer to title please.) But it's 65 degrees so who cares. Not I. I take the shuttle from the airport to the bus terminal in San Jose. All this with never-used high school Spanish. My 40th reunion was years ago. Need I say more about my fluency? Once we pick up more passengers in Cabo, we are on our way. There are five of us on the very large bus. We have seat assignments. I have a seat partner. That's okay, there is a TV screen one seat in front and a movie comes on: *Derailed.* (See title.) English with Spanish captions. I start studying my

Spanish. We arrive in Todos Santos at 8 p.m. My sweet friend is there to pick me up. I arrive at my cozy, quaint, adorable casita at 8:10. I am asleep by 8:30.

I am in Baja.

I Can't Locate Myself

Is how I identify myself, validate me, through where, how and with whom I locate myself?

Have you noticed when going alone someplace totally unfamiliar, how we strive to quickly locate ourselves? Like with maps, for instance? I have always loved them, want to know *where* I am, which direction is north (pilot's daughter that I am).

Where is Starbucks on the map so I can go somewhere 'familiar' to me? Ahhh, I can relax, I know about Starbucks, or my favorite bank.

When I came to Baja, it was very important for me to find my way around immediately. To get the phone numbers of new friends and my landlord written down and in my wallet.

Is quickly 'relocating,' setting up my own internal GPS system, what keeps me from dropping into that hairsbreadth place of 'danger,' of primal terror, of survival, of ego insanity? Of being 'lost?'

Remember a time when you were alone and thought you were lost, whether age six or sixty-six. That's the primal moment of terror I am talking about.

What's that about?

Really.

Again, what comes up for me is having to face that I may not really exist. I don't know where I am. Nothing, no place, no one is familiar. And, who would care about me here, without friends or family, without history?

If I cannot 'find' myself, who am I? What am I?

If I stay in that suspension, in that between-trapeze-bars place, what might happen?

Would I panic? Would I go crazy? What would happen 'then?'

All the 'what ifs'....

I'm just sharing the experiences of my reality. The impossibility of my human condition, of understanding this human being-ness, this it's-just-the-way-we-are-ness.

Again. Can I be cavalier and say, "Okay, ... and ...so what?"

Apparently.

I still find myself 'here,'... and, apparently, functioning.

This living with 'so what-ness' is no small thing.

Stop Trying to Be Somebody

"Stop trying to be somebody."

When I read that years ago in Jean Klein's book, *I Am*, it was like finally being given permission to just stop. Stop trying to define myself, figure out my identity.

Bonnie the teacher.
Bonnie the mother.
Bonnie the daughter.
Bonnie the grandmother.
Bonnie the great skier/dancer.
Bonnie the together one.
Or even just... Bonnie.

Who is that anyway? What does 'Bonnie' mean without all the thoughts, memories, conditioning that make her?

It's back to that idea of 'enough.' Nothing is ever enough if I think I exist. I become consumed. I am a consumer, of everything. But I never fill up because I am not really here!

If I quit thinking about Bonnie, will she cease to exist?

If I don't think about someone, does that mean *they* don't exist?

I don't know.

Maybe.

Probably.

Yes.

But the only way out of going crazy with that one so I don't feel totally alone... and terrified... is to remember that 'I' don't exist either! Remember, I am dreaming.

And, where do we find ourselves in this crazy-making circle?

Back where we started.

This is just an experience, Bonnie. So have it! That's all!

There is no purpose to all this.

Don't try to figure it out.

This is a meaningless place. Don't try to give it meaning.

You'll go ever-lovin' crazy.

I appear to be real.
I appear to have a body.
I appear to do things.

Okay.

So what?

"Just 'have' this experience.

Don't judge it.
Don't solve it.
Don't analyze it.
Don't change it.

Just 'have' it." (Jean Klein)

Computer Crash

Well, it happened.

I postponed backing up, downloading, recent 'stuff,' like iPhotos, iTunes, all my astrological charts, address book, August through December Quicken, some writing. Need I go on? You know the rest of the story.

I was warned. You know that feeling. The flashing yellow light and, 'Bonnie, don't do it.'

I ignored it.

So, I have spent much of the last four days exploring computer repair solutions and practicing a Hawaiian healing mantra: "Bonnie, I forgive you. I'm sorry. I love you. Thank you."

But, maybe more importantly, I have been consciously witnessing my emotional process around all this.

Here I am, twenty-five hundred miles from home, basically dependent upon my computer as a lifeline to my other 'apparent' life as I know it in the States. Skype for talking whenever I need/want to with friends, family, accountant. On-line emailing and banking, for sure.

When I first realized what I had done, how I had cut myself off from my familiar world, my security, my identity, from what defines Bonnie Eddy as a walking, talking, real life human, I had to admit to feeling the base primal terror that was, at least, ever so slightly stirred up in the deep muddy riverbed of my being.

If I cannot instantly contact or be contacted by my daughter, my son, my daughter-in-law, my sister, my friends, those who have defined me (mother, sister, friend)... do I really exist? More of the 'I think therefore I am' stuff again.

There was no longer any easy instant way to get validation, confirmation, that "Hello, I exist."

Don't laugh. This is serious esoteric stuff! The TRUTH even! Back to 'Stop trying to be somebody,' and more.

I just simply was offered another opportunity to look, to have the experience of: I am only consciousness. This is a dream. My body is an illusion. The ego is an illusion. The mind is an illusion. Yet a persistent dream, a strong illusion!

As we speak, I am having a Pluto/Moon transit influence, which means my unconscious emotional security needs and patterns (Moon) are being brought to light to become consciously aware of (Pluto-truth/transformation; the Phoenix experience). Another opportunity to grow, to evolve.

What a paradox! How can I say I don't exist, and simultaneously say I do, that I am having this transit?

It is an utterly impossible situation we find ourselves in. AND, because we are 'in it,' it can not be explained from 'here.' This existence, the idea of body/mind, is caught in the reality of duality, of two; me and any idea of 'other' - other anything: other people, other reality, God as 'not me.'

Excuse me. My landlord just offered to take me to buy a Mexican cell phone!

I exist!

Tell me this existence, this thing we call life, is not crazy. Have heard what we call living described as 'functional oblivion.' Hmm...

Next day.

I am complicating my life, just when I was determined to simplify it. A cell phone. In Mexico. The phone glyphs/prompts are in English; the instruction book in Espanol. Help! I am totally out of control!

Just like the world.

෫෫෫

AND... I bought a tiny piece of property within a week of being here!

Chagrin.

Has been hard to write that fact down. What am I doing? It had just come on the market. A fast sell situation. Best deal around. Another offer came in as I was signing mine.

Can't I, we, just STOP? Must there always be a next project? Is this, too, the ego's vain attempt to perpetuate its existence? Validate it? 'I' bought a lot. Now I have opened a bottomless pit of problems to solve. Problems that will probably keep me validated - 'I' can solve these problems! - and busy all the way out, at this point.

Maybe it's impossible to 'do nothing' here. The ego 'boredom' seems intolerable. What am I to 'do' finding myself in a body?

Have tried saving the world. Tried to end, to abate, pain and suffering. But discovered, it's all me. Save me? Abate *my* pain and suffering? Talk about futile work.

Pema Chodron says, "Abandon hope."

That stopped me in my tracks. I totally resisted the idea.

Initially.

But abandoning hope gets me present, into this moment faster than anything.

Everything just *is*. And will continue to just be '*what is.*'

And then I have to ask myself regarding all my judgments and concerns about 'what is'...

So what?

The Clothesline

Do you have a clothesline?

I do not. Haven't had for years and years since I was a kid.

In Baja, I have a clothesline.

I had forgotten what a sensual experience a clothesline is! Most especially, the removal of clothes from them.

The aroma of freshly air-dried clothing is so delicious that if it was a food we would absolutely crave it!

Tactilely, an aliveness seems present, like eating 'live' food versus processed food.

My relationship to my Baja clothesline has continued to flood me with childhood memories of a tiny mountain town in northern California. Memories of 4H, Brownies, Girl Scouts, swimming in Spanish Creek, biking with my faithful Airedale, Mickey. Spending hours with my friends outside, exploring, imagining. Certainly, not time being afraid of being abducted or worse.

How lucky I was to have had that childhood experience, that 'clothesline' pace of life.

Thank you, God.

Ranger Rick

It's about 10 a.m., still in pjs, having my euphoric clothesline experience. Sitting outside listening to Bocelli on my now-repaired computer, have a delish Mexican cafe latte and fresh fruit with yogurt. What more can I say? If this doesn't inspire me to write, nothing can.

I love my life. I love here and all that it is. Thank you, God. I am so blessed, so very blessed.

Am handwriting this in the same La Paz dollar store 'Star Kid' tablet that I sat and drew house plans in last night, waiting for *Grey's Anatomy* to come on at 10 p.m. At the end I discovered I can watch it tonight at 8 p.m. instead! A much better plan, me thinks. That is, of course, if it doesn't conflict with my active social Friday night plans and the fact that I can only watch what my landlady watches. A dicey game that. Think a Gemini influence must be in there somewhere... she's a channel surfer. Great opportunity to practice detachment: getting hooked into a program or movie and then at some critical moment, the channel switches, often to a *Law and Order* repeat. Ah, yes. Supreme opportunity.

Don't think I have mentioned that in this week's women's tarot circle we talked about our personal numerological year, mine being a seven. Last year a six, about considering lots of possibilities/potentials. This, a year of more contemplation. Gaining understanding of where I have been and seeing a bit of where I am headed. I call this the 'mountain ridge experience,' seeing the paths, trails, roads I've traveled, over other mountain tops, through other deep valleys, to get where I stand at this moment. Standing in awe, actually, in exhaustion, certainly, in utter amazement, in sadness, in joy that I have made it this far.

Shoes still on, body still working, though sometimes sporadically acting out from all the ravaged-fingernail experiences of hanging on, climbing on all fours at times up a mountain side on slipping scree. Three steps forward, sliding two back, carrying a heavy backpack filled with everything a woman needs today to survive: a dependable faith and trust filter, cupped hands to dip into Absolute's always-present golden river of love and light in case the container you're carrying runs out at a least opportune moment. A hidden piece of emergency chocolate - the ultimate 'I am safe' comfort food. Lipstick, blush, in case you're lucky enough to run into a 'Ranger Rick,' (my new nickname for attractive men.) My Montana girlfriends, Linda and Sharon, and I met this quintessential Montana man in the guise of 'Ranger Rick' in the wilds on the east side of Glacier Park on a remote trail. We were left dizzily dumbfounded at how this gorgeous piece of trail candy could have unexpectedly shown up and looked so buffed, pressed, creased and polished coming *out* of the wilds!

I have gotten distracted from the 'ridge experi-ence,' haven't I? Well, 'Ranger Rick' was defi-nitely a distraction!

So, with a durable fingernail file for any future perilous ascent, I stand on the ridge remember-ing all that has come before: divorces, deaths, births, health challenges, successes, failures... and, gratefully, enough joys for a country full of discouraged souls. I cry and cry and cry and cry.

I love. I forgive everyone and myself for what has come before.

I heal.

I adjust my pack full of all I need, find my balance, turn to my future and take my first trusting step on the new unknown path I have chosen.

✂✂

I have conveniently managed to take a slight tan-gent and leave where I was headed in talking about my number seven year with my women's circle.

I really get to see how my mind is so very slippery and conveniently changes the subject when it comes to revealing uncomfortable insights into myself. My behavior habit patterns, exposed.

The group decided to each draw a card which would specifically address how/where focus could/should/might be for our personal year number. Personally, I didn't feel I needed to bother. My focus was clear to me. Simplified: "A determined search, moving forward towards a deeper understanding of the meaning of my life." My ridge experience was a perfect metaphor for me.

So... to draw now a card of how/where one might focus to gain this greater understanding. Risky business, this. I rarely throw I Ching coins or draw a Rune. These ancient interpretative techniques, in my mind, are not to be lightly approached, like a game of Pictionary or charades.

So... thoughtfully, mindfully, trustfully, I draw a card.

The Lovers.

Fuck!

I almost knew it before I drew. (Did I set this up?) This is so up for me. At sixty-five, no, sixty-six as of two days ago, I had somehow thought I would be able to avoid this man/woman thing, live singly in independent, non-sexual bliss.

The Lovers card in tarot represents, fundamentally, the healing union, one's personal union with the Divine and the recognition of the divine within one. These I know about. I can do divine within. However, it also represents forming a loving union with another to increase 'understanding of life' (uh oh), love and commitment, offering significant potential for growth.

If you hear me beating around the bush, you're right. I will get to the juice of this. Give me a minute for courage-building.

For those of you not interested in astrology and Enneagram 'stuff,' you can skip this (or think about exploring these tools - not panaceas - for insight into self; more 'Know Thyself' stuff).

In astrology, I have North Node in the 7th House. 'What I came in to learn' is about being in relationship/in partnership with another. The work is to balance that with 'what I came in knowing' - South Node in the 1st House, how to cover my own back, survive, be independent, thank you very much. So, combining both, it's about loving, interdependent sharing with an apparent opposite in this paradox we call life.

Okay, enough. Not to confuse or overly complicate what is quite simple.

Again, in the Enneagram I am a Counterphobic Six. So! Remembering this behavioral pattern of mine, back to The Lovers.

This November I traveled to South America with a beautiful aware group of men and women on a sacred site tour. Without all the 'story/drama' (another chapter, perhaps), one of the leaders of that tour and I had an immediate connection.

Upon meeting him, I went with him to the Miami airport to pick up two friends, a married couple, who were also making the trip. We had an hour together before they arrived.

One hour.

We shared deeply, soulfully, playfully, timelessly from that 'ridge' place looking from whence we had come.

Laughed at one point til I had to sit on my heel to keep from wetting my pants when he kept feeling a large bug walking up his arm until finally he was unbuttoning his shirt to disrobe! I rolled up his sleeve to discover the tab for rolling up and buttoning a sleeve. Truly, thought I would totally and completely embarrass myself with wet pants.

I have to admit here that my sister and I are some of those rude and strange people who spontaneously and uncontrollably laugh when someone falls down or trips or spills. Am sure it must be a disorder... have not explored that though. But when you see someone sitting on their heel in an airport or on a busy shopping sidewalk in San Francisco, you can be sure they have it!

Back to The Lovers card. (See how easily I distract from this subject?)

Well, this man (let's call him Ranger Rick for ease of conversation and protection of the innocent) and I rocked and rolled with truth-telling, deep revelation and soul searching for two weeks in a situation where he had huge responsibilities to a large group. We had agreed to postpone explor- ing relationship until after the trip. This trip was unspeakably mystical and magical, by the way.

Upon returning, life got busy and complicated with Thanksgiving, new grandbaby and Christ- mas ever-approaching, with the busyness and money all that implies. We did not get together.

But, now I am in Baja.

RR (Ranger Rick) and I have planned a week to- gether here in early February.

And January 26th, I draw The Lovers.

The Universe is frightening, it works so divinely, perfectly, chaotically. Do we really think we can operate outside of it, untouched by that energy?

I don't think so. That microcosm/macrocosm thing. As above so below. You get what you are. What goes around never really leaves (ooh, Bon- nie... now that would be a great chapter!)
Okay, okay. Back to The Lovers.

What am I to say?

Am probably (scratch that), *am* terrified. Of what? Myself? Sex (... which I've said I am not in- terested in? And that may be my truth.) Libido?

Maybe I'm afraid of what we're all afraid of. Love. True, divine love. Loving. Trusting.

Then betrayal? I really don't know what else to say except that the apparent present truth is that I am afraid. AND, I am, yet again, stepping into the lion's mouth anyway.

We, RR and I, talk often and email often. Seem to have a lot to say to each other. Is not boring, an easy connection, especially if I stay present and don't 'make anything up' about anything, 'this-means-that' kind of stuff.

Nothing means anything. It only has the meaning 'I' give to it. How humbling, embarrassing. What a goof I am at times. My active imagination can create scenarios that would frizz anyone's hair. God, help me. Literally, I am asking for help. Please.

Save me from myself.

I'll let you know what happens in February.

Or not.

℘℘

A year later.

I am again in Baja with the time, inclination, and willingness to divulge. Again.

Ranger Rick did come in February. I knew as soon as I picked him up at the bus stop that it was not to be.

The truth?

We are sweet friends.

I think we were sweet friends from the get-go a year or so ago when we had our first connection picking up friends at the Miami airport before the tour.

And.

But.

RR wanted to be married. From the beginning. I knew that. We talked about it. About that I didn't. For sure. Ever.

Maybe we had karma; that's always a good reason to not 'work' something to death. Maybe we were just supposed to say hello. For a minute. Say hello. I love you. I remember you. Hello.
But, not hello, let's get married.

Just hello.

We had a good week. An honest week. A painful week. A sweet week.

We did a lot of work together. High communication. High level of difficult and necessary truth telling. It was a very good thing, for both of us.

And we watched the whales together every day. A healing, perhaps.

We are still very good friends. RR got married. Not long after Baja. He is happy. I am happy for him.

In fact, we are trekking in Bhutan together in a few weeks.

Isn't that wondrous?

☙❧

And.

I am thrown back into myself. My truth. With another Ranger Rick.

It is hello.

But, not hello and let's get married.

I can do that.

It is simple.

Fun.

Easy.

Comfortable.

Showing itself every moment. Nothing made up. No name given to it. No limiting it by naming it, defining it.

No agenda.

Just whatever it is. For as long as it is.

Ahhhh... now this works for me.

Why 'More?'

Dang!

He wants MORE.

It changes everything.

Now I feel I have to armor, defend.

When we find something, someone, someplace we really like, why isn't enough enough? Why do we feel we have to have MORE? Is the human condition that naturally addictive?

I need to see you, touch you, MORE.

I need one MORE beer, cigarette, piece of chocolate.

Why wouldn't one-perfect-piece-of-chocolate experience be enough? Having another is the same experience. AGAIN. And again. Can't we all relive that experience in our minds? Can't you? Remember? Even the taste, temperature, texture... all the sensations awakened by that piece of chocolate. Right now? Relive it?

Without the piece of chocolate.

And, the same with relationship... Relive the sparkling eyes, the velvet touch, the juicy energy of nearness and connection.

Without the person.

We can. Without needing the literal 'here now' experience.

That way there is no attachment. There is no 'possession'... for fear of losing. Something. Someone. Someplace.

As soon as I feel someone wants to 'possess' me - and I'm sure it is out of fear of loss, fear of 'I have to control this or I will lose it' – I'm outta there.

I gotta be free. Because I *am*. *We are*. In reality. I have to be free in 'this' reality, too.

I think of toddlers clinging to their one favorite not-to-be-lost stuffed animal, or blanket, or pacifier. We must be born with the fear of loss, the need for the *constant* experience.

If we can't relive experiences in our minds, we would forget those who have apparently died before us. How is that reliving any different from reliving the evening you just spent? If you want 'more.'

There is only an apparent now. And that is fleeting. I once read that now is only the intersection where the past and future cross, with the amusing caveat that neither actually exists! Where does that leave us in terms of wanting more of *anything*?

Nothing is going on. Nothing is happening. Not really. If I quit having thoughts, what would exist?

These thoughts, this writing, brings me back to the truth for me that this is a dream. I am dreaming.

Imagining. Thinking. Creating. Every moment. If I want the experience, all I have to do is think it. Make it up. Or re-member it, put its members, its parts, back together. And spend some time with it.

I mentioned somewhere before but need to again - for *me;* for *me* to re-member - that we are consumers. I am a consumer. And I keep trying to get full. Like eating too much at a meal. We are way full for a couple of hours, maybe uncomfortably so, but before long we begin to feel empty again. And want to feel full again. The idea that we can never get filled because in actuality we do not exist makes total sense to me. Think about it. I mean really. Doesn't it? I keep consuming and consuming and I will never get full because I am trying to fill an endless vacuum.

One more, of anything, will never be enough. Never 'fill' me.

If I just quit. Consuming. Thinking. Dreaming. Imagining. Would 'I' be full? Would 'I' *be*? Would 'I' end?

Hmmm…

⊗∝

Regarding love. When it's 'more' then it becomes 'special' love.

Special love has unspoken demands, expectations.

"I love you *specially*." Now you give *me* something. Something more.

The content is love. Why can't it just remain love. Period. Without expectations of anything more.

Just simple. Pure. Sweet.

I don't want to armor, defend. From love. From reciprocity.

Maybe it's not: "Let's hang out and not get married."

Maybe it's: "Let's hang out and not fall in love."

If love is all that's going on.

All that we are. All that I am.

Wouldn't that work?

"Let's hang out and not fall in love?"

Because love already is what is?

I'd like to try that.

And see.

Hotel California for New Year's

Good grief! Never, never could I have dreamed this one up.

Plus, with a man! A very young nice looking man. Almost nineteen years younger, as a matter of fact.

Let me back up. On December 30th, I fly from a white 12 degree Montana morning to a green and blue 78 degree Baja afternoon. (God, help me remember that I need to do so every January!)

Enter 'Ranger Rick' (again, to protect the innocent), a guy down here who supplements his income shuttling individuals to and from the Cabo airport. (This is a wonderful thing and definitely beats shuttles and buses.)

RR picked me up and we had an easy laughter-filled drive back up the coast. We said our thank yous and goodbyes and Happy New Years.

The next day, New Year's Eve day, my friend and landlady, Linda, drives me to another friend's to pick up the car I rented last year and am renting this year. The car's battery is dead. The housesitters have no cables. Linda and I drive over to RR's for help. Rangers are ever helpful, right?

He is home and has cables. And three dogs, being a soft touch for these homeless Mexican animals. He is a nice guy. So. He is going to drive me to my car and Linda is going to go home. She gets back in her truck. Her battery is dead. Are we in the right place, or what?

RR jumps her truck and we go get my car. He jumps it and I follow him a ways. The first stop sign, the car dies. He turns around and jumps it again. This time, he will follow me awhile, just to make sure it's charging.

We get separated. Don't ask. This is Mexico.

I go to my tiny lot, purchased on a whim last year while I was here. Then I go to El Sol for groceries, leave the car idling, and, of course, therefore, keys in it. I collect some basic groceries and pay. I seem to have forgotten all my fundamental Spanish. Can't converse at all. I must take a class in Montana when I get home! (Did I say that last year?)

I come out of the store. My car is still there. Trust is the operative word here. I go back by the lot, no RR. So I go by his house to let him know my car is okay, it seems. He is not there. I leave a note in his gate. He shows up. Laughing. I back up so he can open his gate. My car dies. Again, right place. Synchronicity. Or at least good luck. We laugh hilariously and he jumps the car.

As I am thanking him, he leans in the window and asks me if I would like to go to Hotel California with him to celebrate New Year's and his January first birthday. Now there's a line. But it was true!

I say, sure. We crack up.

I love to laugh. I miss laughing. I need to laugh. A lot. This works.

I spend the next forty-five minutes running errands, like buying minutes for my Mexican cell phone, more groceries, all the while leaving my car running. Mexico continued to redeem itself. My car was always there.

RR picks me up at 8-ish and we head out. I haven't gone out for New Year's in more years than I can remember. In fact, I haven't gone out on a date in more years than I can remember. The other Ranger Rick who came to Todos Santos last year doesn't count. I don't know what that was. A date, it was not.

We have great shrimp for dinner at a quaint restaurant. Hotel California was booked for dinner on short notice. Just as glad; was packed with maybe 200 people? We got there for the festivities. Fun bands were playing. The energy is joyful, up. We laugh. Lots.

I have forgotten how to be a woman who is with a man. What does that mean, anyway? If anything ... No, scratch that. It doesn't mean anything.

Just like everything else. I can only be me any-more. Is a relief. Is new. Is, at times, awkward.

But the prevailing feeling is that nothing really matters. Including me. RR smokes. I didn't know that. It didn't matter. I have no attachment to him. To smoking. To drinking. To an attentive arm or gesture.

Maybe I'm just present now. Without projecting into the future or past. Maybe I'm not here any-more. Don't exist.

We watch the fire dancers. Fascinating, strong, graceful young men and women. Contemporary gypsies, beautiful and liberated. Later they come in dancing on stilts. Whimsy. Delight. Play.

We laugh and laugh. At them. At other party rev-elers becoming more and more primal with every margarita. At us.

There were moments when I felt uncomfortable. Out of place. Old. But I just stay with me and these feelings pass. I passed my old self, my old ways of being.

There's nothing going on.

Have fun. Do what you do. Nothing more. Laugh. Dance. As much as you can. Have champagne. Watch fireworks on the roof of Hotel California on New Year's.

Prefer what the universe prefers. Try that.

Even if you are nineteen years older than your date.

Why not?

So what?

Who cares?

Twisted Toes

I am in Baja. I just polished my toe nails. The polish smeared all over my toes because they are no longer straight! When did that happen? Gray pubic hair was plenty enough shock along with gray eyebrow hairs. And now this. What else did my mother not tell me? Remind me to tell my daughter, Shannon, about all this.

P.S. While reading out in the sun, I discovered three two-inch-long white hairs on my right arm!

Good grief!

Edgy Shrimp

Well.

I think the relationship with **RR** is over.

It was sweet.

Til he poisoned me.

With shrimp. That "might have been on the *edge*..."

'Might' have been? Who does 'might have been' with *edgy* shrimp? Or chicken? Or lettuce?

Edgy nuts. Maybe.

So how do I respond to this 'slight error in culinary judgment' after that endless hazy yet oh-so-vivid memorable night, post-dinner, being turned inside out, in intimate relationship with the 'great white bowl?'

"Oh, that's okay-y-y-y."

I don't think so. Not at sixty-six. Sixty-seven in three days. Not with all that seasoned life experience. Wisdom. Cronedom.

"Ackkkk! Are you ever lovin' nuts? You idiot! You gamble with my sweet little body? My sweet little soul? Our sweet little connection? If you are that unconscious, that cavalier, forget it. Adios! Sayonara!"

(I wish.)

"Ya know, there was a flashing yellow light going off as I ate them. But, I overrode the warning. Again. And again."

That's my response??

At almost sixty-seven years old? When do I stop being Pisces-rising 'nice?' And jump into blunt kickass Sag Moon and Mars, if not now? "If not now, when?"

The truth?

No matter what?

It wasn't okay.

And I should have said so.

Certainly, at least, for the sake of other shrimp-loving unsuspecting "I'll try this relationship stuff one-more-time" know-better crones.

Alas. He's another regular ole' vulnerable, well-meaning, foolish, indecisive, fallible human.

Just like me.

It's me. It's me. It's me.

Again.

This is really beginning to feel like that 'one more experience of male relationship' that I don't need to experience anymore. Shrimp or no shrimp.

Is that what happens as people (we, I) age? Finally, it doesn't matter anymore? Enough is enough? The 'new' experiences we used to want we now realize aren't new at all? I'm in another, the same, squirrel cage?

Have thought of the elderly who move away from their homes, their towns, their states into assisted living near their children. Especially if their siblings have died, their old friends have died. It's as good as anything else? It doesn't matter anymore? Nothing matters? Except the love of those who care? Or don't? Such a crazy, crazy, sad, sad place this is. Or not. Another one of those "that's just the way it is here" things?

"You can only watch the same movie so many times before you fall asleep, no matter how 'good' it is." A wise friend's words.

Only buy one more helicopter.

Have one more relationship.

Eat one more edgy shrimp.

Stretch

Oh m' God. I've done it again!

That Counterphobic Six thing. Stepping into the lion's mouth. Again.

Maybe this is my 2008 'outrageous event?' Just four days into 2008!

I have been carrying around a card that says, 'To be free of the need for security *is* security.' That has been my most recent practice. To help embolden myself. And today upped the ante for sure.

I went to Hotel California, a place where you can receive and send faxes here in Todos Santos, and signed a counter offer acceptance contract for 128 feet of frontage on a gorgeous Montana river. With a family of eagles nested in a tree across the river on state land! Oh m' God! I had seen it just before leaving Montana for my Baja trip. I decided to make an offer and then just let go. See what happened... What happened is that I now own it!

Stretch. Stretch. I can almost tangibly feel my self literally stretching. I can't find where that's occurring, like in my body. But it is occurring. Someplace within me.

This property, when I walk onto it, I melt. Ahhhh. The energy is wondrous. The sound of the river. The majestic eagles. The wind in the trees. The surrounding mountain ranges, now crowned in white. The clean fragrant water constantly washing away my tension, my unconscious concerns.

The small cabin on it needs to be totally gutted and renovated. That's okay. I can do that. With the help of friends and trusted professionals. Nine hundred square feet of welcoming sanctuary it will be. Or maybe a permanent residence some day? Like my old Mt. Shasta house, a healing, resourcing place for, and from, friends and family.

I am living my life with more and more courage. With more and more 'who caresness.' Why notness. So whatness. (Like having fun with a man nineteen years younger.)

What's the worst that could happen?

I could sell my current house if I need money. I wouldn't sell the river property. It came to me, 'affordable' (a relative term, I know). But I know I could not replace it. Not for what I paid for it.

Maybe this book will be a best seller? And I won't have to worry about it.

Why not mine?

Why not?

Why not the miracle?

Anything can happen at any time.

Thank you, God.

I Hate It!

Am sitting on this gorgeous beach in Baja. No one to be seen in either direction. Late afternoon. Stunning. Beautiful.

I notice a pelican floating awkwardly in the near waves. Strange. Alone.

Soon he manages to ride the waves into shore. He is not a surfer. He is out of his element. He struggles. Struggles and struggles. Finally out of the surf. His right wing is badly broken. He keeps moving, struggling, to get higher up on the beach as the tide begins to come in.

He sits about fifty feet away. We commune. In spite of my old fear of birds. I tell him how sorry I am. Like when I had to put down our German Shepherd. The pelican, like that dog, knows how sad I feel. I can just tell. But that doesn't help much. I even called a friend to see if anything could be done, knowing as I made the call, it could not.

These are the times when I hate it here. Hate that there is death here. A food chain here. Survival of the fittest here.

"That's just the way it is."

Fuck It.

I don't care.

In my world there would be no death. No killing. No duality. No polarity.

It is times like this when I am so challenged by the idea that this reality is a dream, an illusion. That there is really only one thing going on and that that is love, omniscience, divine intelligence, God... under any name.

Is that why I feel such pain? The pain this pelican feels? He knows his fate. I can feel it with him. Drowning? Dogs?

I can't say SO WHAT? to this.

I'm sorry. I just can't.

I hate it.

It sucks.

∞

I need to get out of my fear of popping out of here, out of this reality.

Be in the world, but, definitively, not 'of' it.

Wake up.

Not go back to sleep.

Live in that reality, that consciousness, that I know is one breath away.

⳥

Moses' one rule: Just don't kill each other.

We haven't learned a thing.

I *have* 'abandoned hope.'

Again.

⳥

We're given:

just enough joy,
just enough pleasure,
just enough fun,
just enough compassion,

to 'make it.'

A few moments and then back to the game. Like serving an ace in tennis... *just enough* to keep one playing the game.

Just enough to forget the struggle, the suffering, the pain, of this place.

I'm sorry. It just doesn't justify perpetuating myself to save the starving, stop genocide, fight crime, say no to drugs.

It's honorable.

But futile.

It will be this way all the way out of this experiment of 'other.' This human experiment.

Jesus tried. So many tried. 'I' tried. 'You' tried.

We have failed.

The human species is just too mean-spirited.

⊗⊆

The next day...

Went to the beach again today.

As I approached 'my' spot (creature of habit that I am), guess what I saw in number..... at their repast?

Buzzards may be the grossest, creepiest birds alive. Ugh...

And, of course, guess *what* they were feasting upon?

I know.

I understand how all this works here.

I understand 'this is just the way it is.'

I *still* hate it.

Today.

It *still* sucks.

Today.

And I *will*, it *will*, tomorrow!

Damn!

Goodbye, Goodbye, Goodbye

I flew from Montana to California to close on the sale of my father's house. On the flight down from Seattle to Sacramento, the plane flew on the west side of the Sierras so I could perfectly track old haunts and memories.

There was Brightenbush Lake where Shirley and I had first connected with Danaan Perry and Earth Stewards. The cascading natural hot pools for soaking. The drive in her convertible through green, green Oregon with its many lakes.

Then Ashland. Often a retreat for me. I would go up, stay at the refurbished Ashland Hotel downtown, go to the movies, a play, possibly shop, or walk through Lithia Park. A getaway from the powerful mountain I lived at the base of, in Mt. Shasta. It was a brief respite from the mountain's cathartic energy, to seemingly hide for a moment. Catch my breath.

Then we flew over the east side of Mt. Shasta itself. I was flooded with memories of the years of week-long Level Fours with Aspire (a spiritual organization that sponsors personal growth retreats). Weeks of solitude, silence, fasting, 'catharting' deep unconscious emotions. The mountain graciously accepting all - the fear, the anger, the frustration - taking it all from me. Experiencing the knee-dropping locomotive deafening power of 'what is,' always, that mystery of the omnipotent. The spacecraft that came and hovered by my ridge point camp site and then flashed back out to the distant desert. I had been watching it for hours, inviting it to come and 'beam me up'... if friendly.' Maybe it did?! The elk, was it really real? Scaring me awake by pounding, rutting, right in front of my tent where I had crawled out to pee. Light, like July 4th sparklers, racing to catch up with Ginny's feet as she walked the meadow below my perch at dusk. The storms, the snow, the One. Thank you, God, for all of it and more.

I think I am saying: "Goodbye."

Goodbye to that time of my life, to Mt. Shasta, to Black Butte, to my friends there. Feels... just... 'over.' I am moving on, into a new life, into a new way of being... on all levels. Into me, my true self, the self without all the conditioning. We fly by Shasta Lake, by Redding, the airport where Dad's office was. I could spot the area where Dad's house is, too. It is in escrow. Finally, a true closure. An end to California responsibilities. I track the river through Red Bluff, then east of Chico I can see Chico State where I went to college in the late 50's. That whole life flashes through my being, gestalted. The loves, the pains, the joys, the friends. Memories, memories, memories.

Goodbye. Goodbye. Goodbye. Thank you all. I love you. Goodbye. Goodbye. Goodbye.

I see my sister's ranch. So many, many memories. Harvest pig parties, weddings, the fertile yeasty smell of the earth.

Then Sacramento, and touch down. Upon arriving I spend a Sunday lunch with three wonderful friends at the Tower Cafe, outside... glorious warm day. More memories. Years with Aspire, growth, craziness, gratitude.

Ginny, inspiring for her 'Hope Rising' project in Jamaica. Patti, still wishing her life was different, her Capricorn nature resisting change. Mardi, sweet Mardi, with her twenty-acre horse ranch run on a courageous shoe string. Three jobs to be able to stay there and keep her horses, her true love. I spend two more days with her, talking endlessly, going to her college classes with her, these classes in sociology, in ethnicity, witnessing her expertise as a teacher, her ability to model feelings and pull her students into her and their hearts, to experience emotions, experience the reality of where we find ourselves. Will I stay at her ranch again? I feel not.

Goodbye. Goodbye. Goodbye. To California? To this enormous chapter in my life.

Shannon, my daughter, and I have five hours together at dinner. Can she get more beautiful? Inside and out? Seems so. Her passion could never hide, be hidden.

I spend several days with my sister. We just do what we do. Deliver pluots, go to Costco, talk and talk. Is good. This reunion. We are so different and yet, not so, yes?

My life is simplifying. Love, give, shine. Everything is as it is. Perfection. Nothing, nobody, needs to change. Surrender, allow, accept, embrace. It all sorts out... on its own. Just be me. Be vigilant against the 'not' me.

While at my sister's, I think I slipped in that category. I went to a dermatologist regarding a skin condition. Ended up doing a way extensive procedure, a dermafill, filling up the lines in my face to lessen crags, ravines. Inwardly, there was a flashing light. I ignored it. Overrode it. Went to my mind for advice, for a decision. Always, always, always a mistake. Always.

Yes, I spose I look 'younger,' but I truly looked younger anyway, because my 'energy,' my attitude, is alive, not dead. Positive, hopeful, looking for the good even in light of knowing futility. (Silly me!)

So, I now have a year or more for this gel to dissolve to get my *real* face back. Others probably won't notice, once the bruising goes away. I look in the mirror and miss seeing 'me.' Me with all my creases and irregularities, all the evidence of my life struggles... and joys.

Goodbye. Goodbye. Goodbye.

If it is all perfect, this, too, must be? Goodbye to old ways of being. Goodbye to trying to ever, ever, ever be someone I am not. This, a lesson hard-learned. What could be more unnatural, unreal, than squirting gel under your skin with a needle, over and over? Jesus! Help!

Okay, Bonnie. "I forgive you. I'm sorry. I love you. Thank you." (A Hawaiian kahuna's advice/mantra for anyone, for any situation.) Over and over and over again. A mantra I need right now. To heal my mind. To move on.

Isn't that all of life... much of life? To move on? Especially the moments of life where we make apparent mistakes, apparent poor choices for ourselves?

"Only good comes." Oh, how I must trust that.

More later on 'lost face.' Or not.

I went to Mt. Shasta for two nights. Stayed with a dear friend, Beth. I didn't want to see anyone else this trip. If you see one, you need to see/call many. We, too, just hung out, talked Human Design, watched movies, watched Michelson beat Tiger by two strokes. Went up on the mountain.

I do miss the mountain, the energy of it, the forgiveness/acceptance of it. It's omniscience. Glacier Park definitely has God presence, too, and it is just different. Maybe it's the history and intimacy I have with Mt. Shasta. The mountain is an old, old friend.

Being in Shasta, as in Sacramento, Chico, was *not* being there and paradoxically, never having left. I think I am finally just 'being where I find myself' and simultaneously experiencing that I am never 'anywhere!' What can I say? Maybe I have already died and don't know it! Just a ghost visiting 'old haunts.' Again, I have the feeling I won't be going there again.

Goodbye. Goodbye. Goodbye. Thank you for all of it.

I met with the realtor, Mike, a true rare sweetheart of a man. We were able to speed up paperwork and walked next door to the title company to sign final papers. I got a very low price for Dad's house, but, of course, it has to be perfect, yes? And truly, I do feel that. ('Not self' versus true self stuff.) It is the new owner's turn to receive what they didn't expect to get, to enjoy the sweetness, the privacy, the tree house experience of that property. Mike: "You're not going to go by, are you?" He is very perceptive, understanding. "No, I'm not. I have already said goodbye."

Goodbye to memories of visiting from D.C. when the kids were toddlers, swimming in the pool, boating on the lake. Returning to that house when I got divorced and left Idaho. A haven til I could get my bearings. Returning every weekend from Sacramento where I was living, teaching, doing workshops, to be with, to help Mom as she struggled with lung cancer. The intimacy she and I shared that, yes, she was dying. Sharing anything and everything I had heard or read about the process of dying. Her gift to me. Mom's subsequent death, the memorial, my former husband coming down, an old college sweetheart coming up. Poignancy.

Then the years from May of '91 to Dad's death in February of '06. Those fifteen years of getting to know Dad. And, finally, regular weekly sojourns staying with Dad at the house several days at a time.

The burden the house became. The first real estate listing, not Mike, craziness. The break-ins, the suit. The relationship with the caretaker, the eviction, the re-listing. What was all that about? Dad not ready to let go? Probably me not ready to let go. (How easy it is to project, yes? Chagrin.) Karma? Letting go lessons? Money lessons? I don't think I will ever know. That's okay. I can let go, move on. Not have to figure it out, carry it along with me into this moment, into the apparent future.

Again, it is what it is. Was what it was. I do not have to revisit it again. I do not have to revisit the house ever again. Redding. The business. It is closed. Finished. Complete. No longer part of my identity.

Goodbye to those old memories.

Goodbye. Goodbye.

Who am I without that identity? Not the dutiful daughter. Not the helicopter business co-owner. Not the aging caregiver. Not the Mt. Shasta perfect house builder. Not the *Black Butte* book author. Not the *A Course in Miracles* sponsor/teacher. Not the workshop facilitator. Not the instructor. Not the life coach. Not the astrologer. Not the Aspire team leader. Not... self.

What an adventure. Who is she?

Really.

How exciting to know I am finding out. AND, that is doesn't matter.

Goodbye, Bonnie.

Whoever you are.

ᘓᘔ

P.S. The dermafill started dissolving by early December. Two months (and $2,000) later, not one-and-a-half years! By March, I had my old natural 'Sharpee' face again.

Hello, my old friend, Bonnie.

Unbecoming Bonnie

My reality, this physical reality, is more and more becoming less and less. I am beginning to feel like a ghost figure. Instead of this world feeling/looking like a movie set as in the past, it now is much less tangible, much less solid, more dream-like, more apparition-like.

The concept that this is just a dream, an illusion, has been with me for years now. But something is shifting. From concept to experience. Really.

Went to a dinner last night. I was looking forward to some social connection. But I was a ghost there. They, too. When I was asked, "What have you been doing, Bonnie?" And I heard myself reply, "Oh, I've had some company and I've started to do some writing." Nobody heard me. I don't think anyone is there anymore. Including me. Nobody really cared what I was doing. Each person was in the squirrel cage of his/her own mind. Including me?

Each apparent person creating his or her own individual, and at the same time, collective, dream... but not 'really' interested in anyone else's dream. The *hero* of his or her own dream as *A Course in Miracles* would say. That's what we do here. And 'I' am always the center of it... whoever the 'I' happens to be... which is each apparent one of us.

My dream is starting to break up.

My son came by last night shortly before I left, to pick up a meat thermometer for the Thanksgiving turkey. Was great, as always, to see him. I love him so. While he was here, Jimmie, the 80-year-old awake healer I've been seeing, and whom I love, called. I had gifted him and his wife John Kent's manuscript on the teaching of Richard Rose. He had just had time to get into it, was on page 35, and called to talk about it. Was such a sweet surprise and so wonderful to have an awake mind to share with, banter with, ask questions of. He reaching down the ladder to assist my ascent. I'm sure of it. And grateful for it on this Thanksgiving Day. My son witnessed much of this conversation. I wrote him a quick note telling him who had called. He heard me sharing with Jimmie: "Jimmie, this reality is becoming really difficult to be in. I struggle with being here, in this craziness, this make-believe place." I am remembering as I write this: The less I believe in anything, the more I feel, intuit. This is true. Was sharing with Jimmie that I had been seriously practicing watching my state of mind and backing away from it. Trying and not trying to 'unbecome what I am not,' as Rose says.

All this and more in the presence of my son, who has on occasion been so disenchanted with life (who of us hasn't?), standing there witnessing until he needed to leave. I loaded my car and left, still talking several minutes with this healer, this friend. He ended the conversation saying that he would like to call in a few days and talk again. I am soooo grateful.

I called my son from my cell. We talked a short time about Jimmie's call. My son relating listening to a recent PBS program about some of this, not remembering the speaker, but saying he will look it up. I welcome this investigation... open myself further to availability... to him, to myself.

Few people want to talk about, hear about this waking stuff. Not the 'feel good,' 'blissful peace' stuff but the hard, scary, unknown stuff.

Near the end of the Kent manuscript Rose says, "Make violent effort, but do not disturb the sleepers." Maybe the sleepers actually are the adverse forces, talked about, not only in this manuscript but in many esoteric works.

This is solitary work. A lone wolf journey, with only a few others in the pack for support, to encourage each other to keep on keeping on. To go *further*. To go further into the unknown.

This dream is literally starting to fall apart for me. Shadow figures we all have become. The teachings talk about 'Reality knows me. Reality will come and claim me, take the final step, when it is the right time, the safe time for that to happen.' So much of the teaching is about the fact that it is already predetermined. All of it. That the final ego - which is necessary for the process, for the keeping on - the final ego is taken from us. This had to be that 'and God will take the last step,' 'of this I cannot speak.' Because it is truly mysterious. It would have to be. It is not of here. It is the unknown. The final journey, adventure.

Or not.

☙ℭ

'Safe' time.

I am beginning to suspect that the safe time has to do with my ability, on all levels, to really take in – I mean *really, really, totally* - that Mitch, Shannon, 'my flesh and blood,' do not exist. *Really.* That they never did. They were never really born. Nor was I. I intuit that there has to be a great deal of preparation within whatever my consciousness is, to prepare me to leave a lifetime of believing this story of Bonnie and her life, her beloved children, for God's sake. None of it is real. None of it exists. None of it is here. 'Here' is not here. There is no here. There is nothing. (But even in this moment, I intuit that 'nothing' – true reality - is juicy?!)

While at the Endeavor Academy in Wisconsin (founded on *A Course in Miracles*) one of my major and utterly shocking epiphanies during one of the lectures was that my kids, my dad, my sister did not exist. I was shocked into a state of being that lasted hours. Hours during which I could do nothing. I could not move. Sat in silence, in light, for at least three hours when someone, who had been left to shepherd me, touched me to bring me out and helped me to 're-enter.'

That experience, like similar others, has never left me. Not just the concept, but the experience of peeking at Reality for just a moment, an eternity.

When would it be *safe* to 'get that' in all its totality? What would it mean? How would it look in this apparent here? Would I be rendered incoherent, inoperative, 'here?' I talked to Jimmie briefly about that. I am beginning to really get that this awakening can, must, take lifetimes. That finally, in the right apparent lifetime, we have progressed enough to be able and ready to 'take it all in,' to be able to handle it. To be able to still somehow 'be in this world' for a minute, fully knowing we are not. Just playing out this last ego life to its natural end.

That when we fully awaken, the final ego is definitely taken from us, and therefore, because it is the ego that thinks all these lifetimes are real, it is the ego that had created all the karma, believing itself and the karma to be real. It is the ego that keeps us thinking we are being reborn from real people, have to clean up existing karma, but actually creating more... on and on. The ego perpetuating this dream, over and over. Different scenery, different stories extracted from the collective.

The endless Netflix of the universe!

BUT. When the ego truly dies... WHILE in an apparent body... the illusion, the dream ends. It's over. We are free from this perpetual squirrel's wheel state of being.

Phew...

☙❧

Am I 'unbecoming' who I am not? Unbecoming being a mother of children? Unbecoming being a daughter? Unbecoming, unraveling the knotted ball of twine that I am? Falling ever backwards into my being until all the story of a 'Bonnie' is used up? 'Uncreating fiction.' Gone. Never was.

Am beginning to really feel the bigness of that. The reality that that is 'in fact' what is occurring.

'Getting used to' the idea.

Preparing.

In the Academy, we used to talk about the fact that all of this has already occurred. And, of course, if all time to going on all the time (Einstein), *this* was my future. And is now. It has already occurred. *This* is how it happened.

Interesting. That is how it feels. I am just watching what has already occurred unfold.

Show itself.

Maybe I just need to throw my arms up in the front seat of this rollercoaster and scream in delight, and terror, at the ride!

Indeed.

Existence *is* a ride... of delight.

Of terror.

Of paradox.

I continue to be 'blown out' by it all.

"The best way out is always through." (Robert Frost)

Bring it on.

It's the best ride goin'.

Pumpkin Pie

I had been reading about Don Beck's and Christopher Cowan's *Spiral Dynamics*, Sandra Maitri's *The Spiritual Dimension of the Enneagram*, and David Hawkins' *Power Versus Force*. All of which are really about waking up. Evolving upwards through waves of ever clearer consciousness. One of the concepts recurring in the literature is the idea that at those higher levels 'fear' ultimately disappears.

I had been doing personal growth work for more years than I would like to admit and THE key growth feature for me personally had been the amount of fear I had been releasing. Now, my rather arrogant 'spiritual' self would like to have thought that I was over fear. Well... right! And doesn't the universe just dish up another test...

I was a member of a wonderful dream analysis women's sharing group, some members of which are Jungian counselors. I loved this group and had experienced so much enlightenment about myself, others, and about just being human. The one thing I didn't do particularly well with when it was my turn to host the meeting, was having a delicious treat for everyone. Many in this group were wonderful bakers.

I realize it's been taking me a bit to get to the point here. So back to fear. I was terrified of bak-

ing. Especially pies. This fear originally was realized at about age fourteen when I made my first
one. That story shall not be shared here.

Knowing the day had arrived to have something
wonderful for our dream circle, I bought the necessary ingredients for a pumpkin pie. I loved
pumpkin pie and think it's a shame that usually it
is only around in November and December...
even though I realize that *is* the traditional harvest time for pumpkins.

I had, during that last year, experimented with
baking pies, largely due to the discovery of pre-
made, and delicious, by the way, pie shells. Making the pie crust was THE worst for me... especially since my sister and all three of her daughters know how to make my grandmother's recipe
perfectly. I had also been working through the
guilt that *my* daughter cannot, of course, bake
my grandmother's wonderful pie crust. So, having finally accepted that I failed pie crust making,
I had moved on. Sort of.

Back to the pie. So that morning after some medi-
tation, breakfast, news, a spa soak, shower,
clean hair and clothes, it was time (allowing myself plenty... our group met at 3 p.m.), to make
THE PIE.

I got all the ingredients out on the counter, had
the oven pre-heated, the pie shell had been out
'resting' to become room temperature. It was
time to open the quarter-folded shell to place it

into the pie dish. The directions read that 'if' the seams crack, put water on your fingers and re-seam them together. I do NOT believe that these seams EVER remain 'seamless' upon opening the shell. At any rate, my heart pounding, the seams seamless enough, I slid the shell into the dish and even though the turned-under edge was thicker on one side of the dish than the other, it looked serviceable.

I began to mix the pumpkin mixture. First I put the sugar, salt and pumpkin pie spice mix together in a large measuring cup and mixed thoroughly and set aside. Then I put two eggs in a large bowl and beat them, 'not too much.' I added the pumpkin and combined well, and finally, I gradually added the evaporated milk. Yes! Ready. However, my mind jumping ahead (no 'presence' in this mo-ment, oh spiritual one), I lifted the still-operating electric beaters out of the mixture. The resulting effect was quite stunning and so surprising that I stood there screaming at the unjustness of it all. All the time, of course, spraying pumpkin all over myself and the kitchen. Finally receiving the neu-ral brain message that it would be prudent to turn the switch to off and end this enlightening ex-perience, I did. Now keep in mind I had started out clean; clean hair, clean clothes. That no longer being the case, I decided to start the much-needed wash. So I stripped down and threw my favorite tunic top and jeans into the washer, wiped what I could from my hair, did a superficial cleanup of the counters, walls, jars of dried nuts and assorted fruits, cookbooks and near windows, and continued.

I was finally ready to pour the mixture into the shell. Hmm. It looked a little light in color. I tasted it. A bit bland. But maybe it would sweeten up upon baking. I poured it into the shell. Yes!! Ta dah! I turned, opened the oven door and happened to catch out of the corner of my eye, the measuring cup with all the spices still quietly waiting to be added. Can't spices talk? Like: "Hey, hey there, I'm over here!"

Thinking quickly on my feet, I dumped the mixture from the pie shell back into the bowl which now had a bit of water in it from being efficiently rinsed for future washing. Of course, I didn't count on the shell obediently following and also splashing boldly into the bowl. I deftly retrieved it, wiping as much of the mixture from it as I could without now adding very wet and movable dough to the whole damn pot! This now is the third screaming episode. The second was upon seeing the missing spices.

Spiritually? I discovered that I had a very active and alive witness who, in spite of 'my' efforts, roared loudly and hilariously at the end of these screaming episodes. That one is probably the one that keeps me healthy through all of this life-changing transformation.

Let's see. What next? Well, 'fearing' (there was that word again), that the AT&T guy might come by to drop off a calling card I was being awarded for being a good Samaritan (another story, another time) and me running around in my underwear, I ran upstairs and grabbed my next favorite tunic top and clean jeans before continuing.

Okay. So. I had one shell left. I had wondered what I would do with it. Silly girl. The box directions said it could be microwaved to soften for placing in the dish instead of another 15 minutes to wait for natural warming. Hmm... the clock WAS ticking. So I bravely did so for the fewest number of recommended seconds. The edges just about dripped! Water, however, was NOT needed on the fingers to close the ever present unseamless seams. Carefully, now being alert to the centering technique necessary, into the dish it slopped. Folding and edging slippery-ily proceeded. Now... would there be enough mixture to complete this task? Fuck it. The clock was definitely ticking and there was not time or, at this point, 'caring,' to go to the store! SO. I poured the whole cup of dry ingredients into the bowl... totally out of sequence now... stirred out as many lumps as possible and poured all into the shell.

Next... carefully, carefully, not to spill... place the pie into the very 450-degree oven. The decision was made not to pull out the oven shelf for receiving the pie because past experience had proved that pushing the shelf back in was indeed a dicey business. The pie was in the oven for fifteen minutes before placing foil around the crust and turning the oven down to 350. Plenty of time to put ice on the top of my now-burned knuckles from the upper oven rack. Mustn't forget to set an alarm for fifteen minutes lest I get distracted. It would be nice to think that I would not need an alarm because I was so-o-o-o 'here-in-the-now' Tao.

The first wash was done now. Just in time to put my second favorite and last tunic top, which had conveniently cleaned the edges of the kitchen counters I had missed earlier, into the wash.

My very observant witness, not escaping the humor of the situation, then kept urging me that in the fifty minutes the pie needed to cook, I should record this experience for posterity. Or something. So having set the timer on the microwave (I hadn't been able to figure out the computerized one on my oven), and for good measure, placed my upstairs alarm clock by my computer, I attempted to recapture this consciousness-raising experience. At least in part.

The two alarms had sounded. The pie, in all of its visual splendor, was cooling on the counter. It was 1 p.m. Plenty of time to clean up the mess, retrieve my first favorite tunic top from the dryer and try to remember the details of the dreams I had conveniently talked myself out of recording in a timely fashion.

Needless to say, I was feeling more human and less heavenly.

But, all was well in my world.

Really.

The Plastic Bag

Yesterday I drove to a town an hour northwest of where I live through the remote mountains to see Jimmie, the healer. I love him. We are friends, always sharing spiritual insights that cross our paths.

I had shared with him, from Richard Rose's teachings: "Are you happy? I am free of happiness." A hugely profound statement to understand and adopt. Talk about detachment!

And he shared with me, paraphrased, that because the Universe is made of 'pure love,' I am totally taken care of. If I relax and simply flow with what is happening, if I remain present and aware in the moment, solutions follow problems, questions bring answers, and all my wants are filled.

This would have to be true because we are one with the Universe, not separate from it! Only one thing going on and I'm it!

Anyway, now being totally healed and awakened after a half hour treatment (ha!), I proceeded to drive my new little Mercedes SMART Car home. Shortly after turning out of the driveway onto a tertiary lane, I ended up first in line behind a mini cattle drive which kept me in first gear and at two to three miles per hour for about forty minutes.

When I left the little town and headed up the hill, I smelled exhaust instead of manure and my muffler was very loud. I pulled over and did a 'preflight,' as my sweet Dad would say, and seeing nothing wrong struck out again. A mile or two further saw an auto wreckage place, the last civilization before home and pulled in because I still smelled exhaust. Two great guys there crawled under the car, as did I, and saw that the header pipe (I'm becoming so 'smart,' like my car!) that connects the engine to the muffler had cracked in half from intense heat!

I proceeded to call AAA, noticing the entire time my demeanor of calm, quiet and clarity about my situation. I then called the dealer in Bozeman who called L.A. and ordered the part overnighted to the foreign car repair that was recommended when I called the guy I had sold two cars to on consignment. All this went click, click, click. Actually, quieter. It was, in fact, seamless. Jimmie's recent sharing entered my mind: 'Solutions follow problems, questions bring answers and wants are filled.' And, it was a gorgeous warm fall day! I also noticed I wasn't happy or unhappy...

It took one and a half hours for the flat bed towing truck to arrive. Part of that time I spent yakking with these great seasoned and true Montana natives at the auto wreckage place. Then I started collecting all my 'stuff,' knowing I would need to take it home when we dropped the car off for repair.

I had soooo much stuff! A vest from the chilly morning trip over, socks from being way too warm now, my huge copy of Rose's manuscript, camera, iPod, recharging cords for it and phone (good grief... where did simplicity go?). Maybe I need to look at the metaphor of all these 'cords?' There was a small journal I keep in the car for jotting down spontaneous insights lest I drive five miles and forget! Also there was some organic jerky and a power bar I just happened to throw in the car, despite my doubt of needing it. It was now 1:30 and guess who was hungry?

I was lamenting that I hadn't kept a plastic bag in the car, for what ever. I mean seriously wishing I had one. How was I ever going to transport all this stuff?

About ten minutes later, I was sitting in the car with the door open, reading, and something caught my eye. Now you must remember, I am out in the boonies. Nothing but this shop is in sight.

A white plastic bag is whimsically dancing like an undulating kite across the highway. It flew between two rows of salvaged autos and passed right in front of my car, hovering there, as it were, waiting for me to catch it. Which I did!

It had no logos on it and it was perfectly clean and unused!

What a fantastical and immediate validation of the way things really are!

AAA showed up. A delightful young guy drove me to the larger town fifteen miles south of mine to the foreign car repair and even gave me a ride back to my house where he dropped me off, toting my perfect white plastic bag full of stuff.

Need I say more?

Besides "Thank you," that is.

Bob and Me

Robert Redford and I are a thing.

I have had an unbelievably wonderful relationship with him. He is incredibly romantic, private, humorous, kind, attentive. Everything a woman could ask for.

Well, duh!

This is 'in my dreams,' literally. I have pretty consistently dreamed of us on and off for a few years now.

Just like in 'this' reality, 'this' dream, I am aware that I am dreaming. I am aware, when with Robert ('Bob' - we're on familiar terms), that I am dreaming and that upon awakening he will *seem* to be gone.

But upon awakening, truly, I wonder which dream is real. Being with him is as real as sitting here writing about being with him. As real as any memory of being with any man. My former husband, my dad, my son, my friends.

When people ask if I am in relationship, it is hard not to say yes!

I have only been unfaithful to Bob once.

John Travolta and I had one brief interlude.

His life was a mess. His wife had left him. He had all these kids and wanted some financial help.

"John, I adore you and I have never had so much fun dancing, but you need to get a grip. Sell your airplane!"

Which dream is real?

Ask me if I care.

What Goes Around Never Left

If none of 'this' is real, and I am really as I originally was... as God *is,* I begin to see that nothing is happening.

'I' make it all up. Wayne Dwyer's 'Row Row Row Your Boat... Life is But a Dream,' stuff.

If I am dreaming, I can only experience what I make up. And everyone in my dream is, of course, me. (Just like Jungian dream interpretation points out.)

Soooo, if there is only me, THEN:

... What you reap you sow.
... You get what you are.
... Love thy neighbor as thyself.
... Giving and receiving are the same.
... Do unto others.
... Nothing can leave its source.
... Know Thyself.
... Like attracts like.
... Love attracts itself.
... I think, therefore I am.

Would all make total sense and be absolutely true, yes?

If there is really only one thing going on and that is *me,* or me as not separate from that one thing, then...

What goes around comes around BECAUSE it never really leaves in the first place!

Oh, m' God.

Synchronicity

I awakened early this morning and could not go back to sleep. *So It Ends* was creating itself persistently in my mind. I finally gave up. Got up. And started transcribing.

It literally wrote itself. Easily. Effortlessly. Almost choicelessly.

Today is my birthday. Was this a birthday present?

I think so.

I think the birthday message is that the book is finished.

Just like that.

I called my daughter as planned so she could wish me happy birthday 'in person,' or at least in 'real time.' (Calling me on my Mexican cell is crazy-making and dicey at best.) She had hoped to be able to come down for a visit but said life was becoming pretty hectic right now and that she just didn't think she'd better come.

I mailed off *So It Ends* to my editor and dear friend. Then called her later as we, too, had planned. I told her the book just felt done. That I even felt done with my Baja time, at least for this year.

She shared that next week the house was hers. Everyone else gone. Why don't you come up and we'll crank this editing out in person and have fun at the same time?

'This' was starting to feel fun!

I checked on flights for a week from now and there was availability and I had miles to use for it.

I went next door to the gal who had booked a flight to Tlaquepaque for five of us for about that same time and told her that the unexpected opportunity to go to San Diego really felt like right timing and I would just eat that ticket. And, this freed up the room reservation problems we had been experiencing with five people rather than four.

She hadn't been aware I was writing a book and we had a fun connection sharing about it. At some point she mentioned photos of her models. I knew she was an artist (living down here part-time, from Alaska), but not that she was a photographer. Wow, I said, can I hire you to take my book photo? (Had not crossed my mind until that moment that that was something I would need to get done.) She replied, let's call it a trade for that astrological reading you did for me last time you were down. How about I come over at 3?

That sweet offer just more than paid for the canceled flight ticket!

Can you feel where I'm heading with all this?

I called Ranger Rick to see if he could take me to the airport on that date.

Sure. But, no shrimp lunch.

The car I am renting is supposed to go to another friend when I'm scheduled to leave four weeks from now. However, she is on foot now and will be thrilled to pay for February and have transportation. This covers half the rental I will be walking from.

My editor's sister will be visiting at the end of our work/fun week and can give me a ride from San Diego to Sacramento where my daughter lives. I will visit briefly there and go to my sister's in Chico just in time for almond blossoms. My most favorite time, my most favorite thing. I will fly home from Sacramento to Montana and return on the scheduled day... or not.

Is this what serendipity, synchronicity is?

What 'right action' is?

"A healed mind does not plan," is?

When the energy is quickened, details are seamless, all is effortless.

And fun.

I revel to the max in this kind of energy when it surprisingly comes.

Is it time to leave Baja for this year?

I think so.

x

Reflections

The renovating of this small cabin on the river has been a total metaphor for what has been occurring for/in me.

A reflection, if you will.

Is your car acting up? Dead battery, perhaps? Generator?

Ants in the house?

Dog biting people? Three-year-old biting people?

Take a look inside you.

Be honest.

Dig.

What's really going on?

∂છ

The cabin has been gutted totally.

Inside and out.

Saved only 'its bones'... its survival structure.

That's *me*.

I'm being stripped of everything that's not absolutely necessary.

Just left with my body to get around in.

All my old belief systems, unconscious habit patterns, shown to me and abandoned.

∞∝

We put the power lines underground. A three-foot deep trench 150 feet long. What was hidden exposed.

In one day we covered that trench and unexpectedly had to dig next to it, a five- foot deep trench for a new water (emotions) line to the house, 170 feet from the well.

A new pump has to be put into the well itself so that water would flow easily, safely, wouldn't freeze. (hmmmmm).

Lots went on for me during this time. Lots of painful, difficult, previously buried and held back emotions.

Experiences with family and intimate friends drew my truth to the surface, regardless of the fear and pain involved.

I was finally so out of integrity with myself, I had to speak up. Say, "*This* isn't okay! *That* has to stop!"

I had to stop being the 'good' one.

The 'good' mother.
The 'good' grandmother.
The 'nice' one.

I had to give up nice for truth.

It wasn't pretty. It was a major mess.

Ugly.

Like the renovation.

Expensive.

But necessary.

I put an 'X' on my hand and daily re-did it to re-mind me that *everything's perfect*.

That *everything* is in my own best interest.

I hated it.

It's like that sometimes when things are true.

∂∝

The ground is covered again now.

New power and water systems updated.

Big windows going in... openness.

The crawl space cleaned up. Mold treated. Gone.

A new floor.

A new foundation.

The roof is coming off next week.

Dare I even think about what that could mean, could bring?!

Ohhh, well...

Bring it on.

It's time.

Finally.

I'm ready.

Or not.

Let's really open things up.

My family, friends, will shudder.

Everyone, everything is affected. Must shift. When we change. When we shift.

And vice versa.

Sweet Water

NEVER lose track of your dream. NEVER.

All of my life, the smell of sweet water has elevated me. More than any other experience.

Yes, even more than sex.

Holding a baby grandchild comes close.

But...

A whiff of sweet water stops me in my tracks.

Always has.

Can remember being a child growing up in a tiny mountain town in Northern California and walking past a creek, driving over the river, living across from Dellinger's Pond. And even at six years old, everything else would stop.

Suspension would occur.

I would be taken out.

Taken in.

'That' was heaven.

Divine dispensation had occurred.

Have asked all my life to live by water that would 'send' me.

And here I sit.

Utterly 'sent.'

What I wanted won over what I truly thought I could ever have.

A miracle.

A home, a life, by living sweet water.

Never lose track of your dream. Never.

Miracles are a breath away.

Maybe years in terms of 'this' physical reality.

BUT, in terms of heartfelt desire?

A moment.

Time has not passed.

There you are.

Like it never wasn't.

And all you can do is be humbled.

And.

Eternally grateful.

And.

Blessed.

Life is a strange and miraculous game.

Play it.

Trust it.

No matter what.

And.

NEVER lose track of your dream.

Never.

Never.

Never.

What is ours comes to us when we are ready.

When to End

It's a rare gift to end anything in divine timing. Even knowing as a speaker, a teacher, when to stop talking... intuit when enough is not only enough... but when something is 'as good as it gets.'

End a visit, end an evening, end a conversation, end a hairdo, end a project. Be able to be present enough to tangibly feel when the energy has shifted and it's time to bring the event, whatever it is, to closure. Before it becomes diluted because of hoping for 'more.'

It doesn't *mean* anything that the moment ends, the particular energy has left.

You just say goodbye and follow the flow of life to what's next.

If we can't let go when we know it's time, cannot detach, if we are not paying attention to the energy all around us always, our soul cannot get us to the next right place for us.

'We' want to control that energy. Make it last longer. Even forever.

We go to sleep.

Miss the signals for right time, right place, right action.

It is a gift.

Knowing when to end.

So It Ends

When Cindee, my editor, had me read to her these stories, these essays, the order of them magically, effortlessly, fell into place. The book was continuing to write itself, show itself. Certainly didn't feel separate from us. It was the experience of one thing happening, one energy.

We both cried and laughed with the reliving of these experiences, these ordinary and extraordinary life episodes.

At the end of those sweet hours, Cindee said, "Ya know, I think its title is: Am I Dead Yet?"

It sounded perfect. We cracked up.

I hadn't realized until then, until the end of reading this little big book, how much about death and dying it literally is. Death of people, of animals, of relationships, of ways of being, of beliefs and conditioning. Figuratively, it was about 'die before you die.' I don't exist. Maybe I'm already dead.

Initially, I was shocked.

Momentarily horrified.

Oh m' God, what have I done?!

But as I said in the introduction, this is my truth. Today. From what I have learned on my journey.

I have gotten to see, through this writing, what my truth really is.

It is no small thing.

And I am so grateful for this experience.

So, sweet reader, you made it.

Through some of 'my' story, 'my' dream.

And that is all we really have, isn't it?

Our story.

And because we are the *hero* of our story, of our dream, it seems to be the one thing that has meaning to us in this horrid, wonderful world.

And.

If this is, in fact, a dream, an illusion, it's not *really* what's going on.

It is a paper tiger.

Poof!

During the years I was involved with a spiritual group that sponsored what I called 'turbo therapy,' I learned that to really heal, to really grow up, become a true adult rather than a large child, we have to drop our story. Certainly our attachment to it.

Let all the drama go.

That remains a truth for me. It humbles the ego.

Which is a good thing.

We are the same, you and I. Anything I seem to do to you, I do to me. When we are our natural selves, the universe takes care of us.

We get what we are.

And that remains a truth for me. Keeps me awake.

Which is a good thing.

So in saying goodbye, if *your* story, *your* dream, seems a nightmare, I invite you to do whatever it takes to change it.

To dream a better dream.

Because you can.

What do you have to lose?

Maybe that you and I might find we were wrong at the end, when we die?

So what?

Wouldn't it have been a more conscious, more kind, more joyfilled way to live life?

I think so.

But, I don't know for sure.

I'm not dead yet!

Or..... am I?

Bonnie's Favorite Books

I have bookshelves full of books I have loved. These stand out as those that seem most memorable. Dependable guides. Healing information. The ones I pick up to remind myself, to keep myself awake. Tried and true books. For me. These are in no particular order. I just grabbed them off my bookshelf.

Adams, Robert. *Silence of the Heart.* Acropolis Books, Inc., 1999.

Chodren, Pema. *When Things Fall Apart: Heart Advice for Difficult Times.* Shambhala, 2000.

How to Know God: The Yoga Aphorisms of Patanjali. Translated and with commentary by Swami Prabhavananda and Christopher Isherwood. New American Library, 1969.

Klein, Jean. *The Ease of Being.* The Acorn Press, 1984.

Klein, Jean. *I Am.* The Acorn Press, 1989.

Shain, Leonard. *The Alphabet Versus The Goddess: The Conflict Between Word and Image.* Viking Penguin, 1998.

McKenna, Jed. *Spiritual Enlightenment: The Damnedest Thing.* Wisefool Press, 2002.

McKenna, Jed. *Spiritually Incorrect Enlightenment.* Wisefool Press, 2004.

McKenna, Jed. *Spiritual Warfare.* Wisefool Press, 2007.

Hawkins, David R. *Power Vs. Force: The Hidden Determinants of Human Behavior.* Hay House, 2002.

Hawkins, David R. *The Eye Of The I : From Which Nothing Is Hidden.* Veritas Publishing, 2002.

Hawkins, David R. *I: Reality and Subjectivity.* Veritas Publishing, 2003.

Harrison, Steven. *Doing Nothing: Coming to the End of the Spiritual Search.* Jeremy P. Tarcher/Penquin, 2002.

Deida, David. *The Way of the Superior Man: A Spiritual Guide to Mastering the Challenges of Women, Work and Sexual Desire.* Plexus, 1997.

Beck, Don Edward and Cowan, Christopher C. *Spiral Dynamics: Mastering Values, Leadership, and Change.* Blackwell Publishing, 1996.

Wilber, Ken. *Boomeritis.* Shambhala, 2002.

Zukav, Gary. *Seat of the Soul.* Fireside, 1990.

Living Your Design: A New Manual for Awakening. Revised and edited by Richard Rudd. Human Design America, 2004.

Kent, John. *Richard Rose's Psychology of the Observer: The Path to Reality Through the Self.* TAT Foundation, 1990.

A Course In Miracles. Foundation for Inner Peace, 1976.

Maitri, Sandra. *The Spiritual Dimension of the Enneagram: Nine Faces of the Soul.* Tarcher/Putnam, 2001.

Sinetar, Marsha. *Do What You Love, The Money Will Follow.* Paulist Press, 1987.

Castillejo, Irene Claremont de. *Knowing Woman: A Feminine Psychology.* Shambhala, 1997.

Hay, Louise. *You Can Heal Your Life.* Coleman Publishing, 1984.

Coelho, Paulo. *The Alchemist.* Harper San Francisco, 1994.

Housden, Roger. *Chasing Rumi: A Fable About the Heart's True Desire.* Harper San Francisco, 2002.

About the Author

Bonnie has been an explorer of consciousness for over twenty-five years. This exploration has changed her experiences of life events. Has created growth and healing from them.

Understanding.

Sheryl Maree Reily

Which has enabled her to pass along this information to others. For many years she facilitated personal growth workshops for both public and college audiences.

She was raised in small mountain towns. Raised her family in a small Idaho mountain town. And, currently, resides near a small Montana mountain town living on a beautiful and inspiring river.

She taught school for years teaching kindergarten through college levels. She and a colleague, Ed Stupka, wrote a secondary teaching manual, *The Right To Succeed*. Jane English (co-author of *Tao Te Ching – Lao Tzu – a comparative study*) and Bonnie wrote, *Mt. Shasta's Black Butte*, a non-fiction and pictorial book of a popular and local mountain.

Mountain outdoor life has, obviously, been a huge part of her experience, although she has resided in Washington, D.C. and other metropolitan cities.